how to get published in
business/professional journals

Joel J. Shulman

how to get published in business/professional journals

A DIVISION OF AMERICAN MANAGEMENT ASSOCIATIONS

Library of Congress Cataloging in Publication Data

Shulman, Joel J   1926-
  How to get published in business/professional
journals.

  Includes index.
  1. Business report writing. 2. Authorship.
I. Title.
HF5719.S55   808'.0666021   79-54850
ISBN 0-8144-5555-7

First Printing

To Helen and Marian

To Helen, my wife of 25 summers and winters,
who tolerated my "disappearance" evenings and weekends
and encouraged me to spend the time to write this book;
and to Marian, our daughter, who devoted many hours
to proofreading numerous drafts of materials
in which she had little or no special interest.

preface

HAVING BEEN INVOLVED for the past 25 years with the business and professional press in various relationships and capacities, first as a contributor and then as an editor, I have become aware that much of the material submitted for publication is ineptly formulated. It is less a matter of poor preparation of the material and its content than of the material being inadequate or inappropriate for the medium and the intended audience.

Some material is prepared by professional public relations personnel under "instructions" from management. It is often so commercial and promotional in tone that it fails on all counts to meet the desired objective—to get published. One is sometimes amazed that corporate managements even permit time and energy to be expended for what amounts to gratification of the egos of the chief executives or proprietors.

The cause of such poor submissions is not the material itself and certainly not any lack of knowledge or ability on the part of the authors. The problem is a lack of comprehension of the purpose and requirements of the business (also called "trade") and professional press. All too frequently, people in business want to utilize the editorial pages of respected publications as a means by which to obtain "free" publicity—really free advertising. Although they would like to think that they are gaining by such exposure, they gain little and lose much. It may be that they are greedy and are trying to "get something for nothing" or they may simply want to present their own points of view with the belief in their overriding importance.

Business and professional publications cannot survive without both financial and editorial support from the industries and professions they serve. Therefore, writers have much to gain by learning what the requirements of these publications actually are and learning how to utilize the services offered by the business and professional press so that they can gain the maximum advantage possible.

It is my hope, by means of this book, to inform those who would write for the business and professional press how to go about doing their chosen tasks better—for their own benefit, for the benefit of the editors with whom they must deal, for the benefit of the readers who will ultimately pass final judgment, and, not the least, for the benefit of those companies and organizations that wish to have their work reflected favorably to an interested, specialized audience of customers and colleagues.

If I succeed, I know that at least one frustration on the part of the would-be writers will be ameliorated, and at least one frustration on the part of editors will be removed. In truth, I will feel that I have succeeded if I just make my own job easier. I know I will receive material for publication that is in better condition, requires less editing, and is directed squarely at the audience my publication serves.

I will succeed if the path of the author is made smoother. He (or she) will have a guide that is direct and specific. He will not need to founder from lack of direction. He will not need to risk rejection of an article or paper after putting in many hours of research and writing. Ultimately, the results will work to the advantage of us all.

It is not without an awareness that I may be implying criticism of some people in the professional public relations community that I undertake this task. On the contrary, 25 years of experience in industrial marketing and publishing has taught me that the professional writer will welcome a detailed and logical exposition of this topic. It will assist such professionals when they have to work with clients who do not have—and cannot be expected to have—a true comprehension of the requirements of the editors of business and professional publications who labor daily in these areas.

For the first-time or established writers, this book sets out guidelines that will be of value. If writers follow the suggestions and maintain an awareness of their ultimate objectives, they will find this book a great encouragement to proceed further.

JOEL J. SHULMAN

contents

introduction

IF YOU WERE TOLD to write an article for a business or trade magazine, what would you do? Would you know how to go about writing it . . . how to go about getting your ideas accepted by an editor . . . how to prepare your materials . . . how to get approvals . . . and more?

If you came up with a good idea—or an idea you thought could be developed—for an article concerning your work, would you know how to find out if the idea was really good enough for an article? And would you know what steps to take to get the idea into a form suitable for publication?

If you work for a company and you have to help an engineer, an attorney, or a scientist to write an article, would you know how to advise him or her? Would you know what you could do to help? Would you know how to negotiate with the editor of a business magazine or professional journal?

Or, if you are a manager and you think that a development of your company or your laboratory is something that your professional community should know about, would you know how to advise the appropriate writer as to how to get published? Would you know how to set up or obtain the necessary support functions to help him?

Chances are that at some time in your business career you will find yourself in one or more of the above situations. Chances are that unless you get deeply involved in writing for business and professional journals, you would flounder about before you "got wise" to the methods that you need to get published. At such a time you could use some advice—indeed, would welcome some advice.

When you want to write on a subject that you feel is likely to interest certain people in your profession or industry, the matter of placing your ideas in words is often the easiest of your tasks. If you are to get your article or paper published, you must understand what steps to take to get the results you want.

This is not as hard as it might seem. What you will be doing is marketing, or "selling," the idea. First you sell it to an editor; then you might get the chance to reach the magazine's readers. If you can't get your idea accepted by an editor, you can't reach the readers. So, if you are to get any benefit from your writing you have to be like a politician. The politician first must get elected; only then can he carry out his program. As a writer, you first have to get an article published; then you can put across your ideas. The two steps are indivisible.

THE CASE FOR CONTRIBUTED ARTICLES

There is much to be said in favor of having all articles in a business publication written by the permanent staff of that journal. There is more to be said in favor of the contributed article, and that is where you can be of service to both your industry and yourself.

For one thing, contributed articles are looked upon very favorably by the most highly regarded publications. Contributed articles do a lot for a magazine's reputation. The editorial package is enhanced by the reputation of the outside expert if the person's name, company, and other affiliations go into the byline.

The greatest advantage of having contributed articles in a magazine is that such articles allow the magazine to provide expertise unavailable from its own staff. This is true whether the contributor's name is on the article or whether he has made some behind-the-scenes contribution. Either way, a contributed article can offer a reader some specialized data that would take much too much effort for a staffer to obtain, assuming that he possessed enough technical knowledge to even begin to try. The cost-effectiveness of such an article would probably be too marginal if it were staff-written.

As a general rule, few editors are really technical experts. Some are no longer actively pursuing a specialty, and others, even though they continue to work in narrow areas of expertise, lose touch, as time goes by, with the details of their specialties. Most editors cannot continue to work in a specialty if they are editing a magazine. In their new work, they learn less and less about more and more.

As will be seen throughout this book, the contributed article might be more accurately called "negotiated" or "contracted," since such articles are usually guided by the editor or written to his specifications. There is still a need for a great deal of guidance and effort on the part of the editor. Nevertheless, even when an editor spends much time guiding an outside author, he will still spend far less time on the article than if he had had to write it himself. This leaves him more time to develop a balanced editorial diet for his readers.

THE CASE AGAINST CONTRIBUTED ARTICLES

There is another side to the coin. For one thing, most editors cannot rely on contributed articles to meet all the requirements of their publications. Some compromises are necessary. If a manuscript that has been submitted does not come up to the writing standards of the publication, it may have to be reworked. If, however, the author is late and the subject has been promised to the readers for a particular issue, there may not be time to rework the material. Both author and publication may be embarrassed by the result.

When contributed articles are paid for, they constitute an extra expense over staff-written material. Of course, they may represent a savings as well, if their quantity and quality enable the magazine to dispense with staff editorial talent.

Balance is often a problem with a contributed article. A contributor cannot be expected to be able to obtain all pertinent data about competitors' products. He should not be expected to provide negative data about his own products, although he may be honest enough to try.

Certain types of articles come out better, or more balanced, when staff-written. A staff editor can write best those articles that require broad knowledge of a field but little technical expertise. These will include news features, case histories, state-of-the-art reports, overviews, and roundups. These same types of articles can often be quite competently written by contributors. Staff writers will not normally do as well with articles of an engineering or how-to nature, explicatory material, or subjects that require specialized technical knowledge.

For an editor, the most distressing part of working with contributed material is his inability to know for certain when he will have the material available for publication. Staff-written material is predictable and controllable. Contributed material is not. If the contributor can offer expertise that is but little different from a staffer's, then his contributed article will not be quite as welcome.

For a contributor to find continued acceptance by a particular editor, he will have to establish a track record of reliability. The manner in which he works with the editor in his first endeavor will be important in establishing this. After that, he will know how to work and the editor will know how to work with him. If the two can establish a good working relationship, the contributor will do well—and so will the editor.

On balance, there is more in favor of contributed material than against it. If an editor can obtain contributed material of a quality equal to that which he can get from his staff, then the contributor is in a doubly advantageous position. An editor can normally expect such quality when material is provided by professional public relations personnel. If what you can give the editor is suitable for his publication, then you will be a "published author." It is an objective worth striving for.

GET TO KNOW THE READERS' INTERESTS

You already know that as a writer you have to meet the needs of the editor. Now put yourself in the position of the editor who has to meet the needs of his readers. You will be doing the job that the editor usually does: writing material to get a particular reaction from a specific group of readers.

So, in addition to the physical work involved, you as the author should also be aware of what writing and presentation techniques will work best. Proper techniques will enable you to convey your ideas most effectively, making the reader want to absorb them. In doing this, you will want to avoid having the editor do a lot of work, particularly if you have selected the magazine in which you want to have the article published. You will probably want to have your own writing style prevail; this is part of the pride of authorship. And you will want to have your message received in the way you intended.

This is a form of marketing your article. This book, in fact, deals only with marketing. Nobody can tell you what to write, nobody can really tell you how to write, and nobody can tell you what audience you want to reach; you have to make certain decisions yourself. These concerns do not arise until you have a subject to write about. The only thing this book can tell you is what goes into planning and writing articles so they will be accepted most readily by the editors you want to impress. This is the "marketing" point of view.

You will have a second, and very important, objective: having the reader respond favorably to your ideas or story. To do these things, you must know both your editor and your reader—not necessarily personally, but you should have a good idea of what the editor wants and of who the reader is and what he is most likely to respond favorably to.

FIND THE JOURNAL

Once you have established the topic you will be writing about and the particular "market" of readers you want to reach, your next step is to find the journal or journals that you prefer to have publish your proposed article or paper. With some very specialized subjects, you, or someone acting to assist you or in your behalf, will have to have a fairly sound knowledge of which journals are best to approach, that is, which will be most likely to accept and publish your article.

Most authors try to place specific articles in particular, specialized publications with which they are already familiar. They generally know that the subjects about which they write are of interest to the readers of such journals. Where this is not the case, it will be necessary for you to embark on an organized and logical search for suitable publication vehicles.

There are many specialized publications that provide de-mographic information on their audiences. For some types of articles you will not need to be concerned about this, but in most situations it will be important to you.

IS THERE A CHANCE OF GETTING PUBLISHED?

As with any venture of some scope and requiring effort, you will be best rewarded if, before starting to write any article or paper, you first determine if there is a realistic chance of getting your material published. When the research and writing efforts you would have to expend are minimal, the inquiry process may take more time and effort than you would need to prepare the manuscript materials; you might as well start writing im-mediately.

For the most part, however, there is very little to be lost and much to be gained by first making a telephone call or writing a letter to find out if the editor would be interested. This holds true whether you are a professional writer, a public relations agent, a free-lancer, or a technical specialist. Nobody wants to do a lot of work that will only be rejected when the same effort could be applied to something else that would pay off handsomely. Be alert to the reality that there are many editors who simply will not accept any material for which prior contact has not been made. And these editors generally control the most desirable publications to have your articles appear in.

In this book, it is assumed that payoff is measured only in getting published. There are some special situations that involve financial remuneration or honoraria to authors, but these are incidental and will not occur frequently. In cases where such payments are made, inquiry is usually an absolute necessity and negotiation follows subsequently.

EXCLUSIVE PUBLICATION

Some editors insist on total exclusivity; the article is to appear in no publication but their own. The stature that their publications enjoy may be such as to enable them to make demands of this sort and make them stick.

Other editors will consider the requirement for exclusivity fulfilled if no competing publication receives the material until they have had the opportunity to publish it first. Defining a competing journal is sometimes difficult, since much technical material crosses technological or business lines. What shall and shall not be exclusive to a publication must necessarily be determined by the editor who is considering publishing your article.

The worst situation for an author to place himself in is to submit his material to a journal that has such low standards it will accept almost anything that is written because it lacks sufficient resources of its own to obtain material suitable for publication. Nevertheless, there can still be some commercial value in having an article appear in such a publication. These journals frequently have very large circulations and correspondingly large readership, although the readers are not very loyal—a matter that may be of little or no concern to the author.

IF THE EDITOR IS INTERESTED . . .

We may assume that the editor has expressed an interest in your article. (If not, let's end our discussion here.) Now you must organize your article, but not yet write it.

The proper form for a technical paper designed to appear in print is different from that of other modes of presentation. Some approaches used for effect in verbal presentations will, if used in written form, alienate the reader within the first few words. Therefore, in organizing or outlining your article, you must be aware that a magazine does not have the ability to "capture" a reader. The reader may stop reading any time he wishes, and you cannot continue to command his attention as you can when you are speaking.

With the objective of enticing your reader to continue reading, you should know the particular type of audience and journal you are planning to write for. Of the two types of publications, business and professional, the business (or "trade") journals usually—and I emphasize the word *usually*, because no rule is perpetually true—are read by people who are generalists in their technical fields.

Professional publications are read for the most part by people who are specialists in their fields. This difference requires vastly different methods of organizing and presenting the subject matter of articles.

Up to this point, the editor's job has been minimal. The primary load has been on your shoulders as the prospective author. Now the workload will begin to shift to the editor. When you prepare your manuscript you must now consider not the eventual audience, the readers, but the editor who must work with your material.

There is no such creature as an editor who has enough time to do the editing that all submissions require. For obvious reasons, the manuscript that comes closest to the version preferred by the editor will be the one that he finds most acceptable for publication. It is also the one most likely to get published in an early issue of the magazine. If an editor has much work to do on your article to bring it up to his standard of quality, he will make certain that his immediate needs are satisfied in order to meet his constant and unrelenting deadlines. An article that is difficult to edit will suffer delays in reaching print; it might even become obsolete.

PASSING A BOARD OF REVIEW

If the magazine has an editorial board that must review manuscripts for publication, the best and cleanest submissions will get the fastest and earliest approvals. Quite aside from quality of content, the manuscript that is easiest to read and best organized will receive more favored consideration.

The editor may have indicated to you only that your idea is acceptable. He will not yet have notified you as to whether your manuscript, as written, has been accepted or is acceptable. If the board, using any criteria it wishes, should conclude that the material is presented improperly, it could disallow publication.

On the other hand, more than one major technological and scientific development has been refused an impartial review because of preconceptions held by members of an editorial board or an editor himself. This is to be expected occasionally; it is a rare and feckless editor who will deliberately upset his readers with new and revolutionary ideas or who will embark on a crusade to bring unpleasant developments before his readers. Such intrepid actions by editors are what awards for journalism, and unemployment, are made of.

WHAT GOES INTO AN ARTICLE?

In preparing your manuscript, the details of your subject matter will determine the tone and manner you use in approaching your topic and audience. A publication such as *Scientific American* uses the first person extensively, without concern that this will offend readers. However, should you as an author wish to report on a corporate proprietary development, you should be aware that editors are very wary of claims, particularly generalized claims of quality that are not substantiated. There are ways to get around some of the problems that this caveat creates. You should consult with the editor if you want to use an approach that is radically different from that normally used in his journal.

Most business and technical publications, and virtually all professional ones, publish illustrations. Illustrations make articles more attractive, more interesting. If it is possible to use an illustration in place of words, the picture may truly be worth a thousand words. In fact, if you can replace the thousand words with a picture, your article may become even more acceptable to the editor.

Therefore, for each article you develop, consider: Are pictures necessary? What types of graphs, charts, photographs, color, line drawings, schematics, cutaways, or exploded views will be acceptable? Who will do the finished drawings and to what standards? This is all necessary to know and establish early in the negotiations with the editor. If there are costs involved, you may have to assume them. Be prepared.

If the publication has a style guide, this is where details concerning drawing and other specifications may be found. Follow the specifications or prepare to receive a rejection. No matter that you are working to a more rigid standard; follow the rules. Very little of business press monies ever go toward redrawing technical artwork. This sometimes happens but is very rare.

ARTICLES ARE NOT THE ONLY MATERIALS PUBLISHED

Not all writing for the business and professional press involves major articles. These magazines publish all types of materials, including news releases. They obtain material from reliable primary sources, from contacts within an industry or profession, from staff members involved in non-editing functions (such as sales and production), and more. If your company wants to have news of its activities published, it should see that its press releases are received by the editor in a usable form and with suitable and complete data.

ARE ADVERTISERS FAVORED?

If you believe that advertisers get special treatment, you are right. This is not, as commonly believed, simply because they are advertisers and advertising pays the bills. In fact, this is very frequently not a factor. Being an advertiser may even work to one's disadvantage in negotiating with an editor concerning an article. Editors don't want to be accused of favoring advertisers. Apparent favored treatment occurs, when it does occur, because advertisers are already known to be committed to doing business with the readers and are, therefore, generally better recognized as being interested in the specialized marketplace. A newcomer to the field has yet to establish his credentials and his dedication to the interests and welfare of the readers.

THE PRESTIGE FACTOR

A published article may have tremendous value to the author's company or organization beyond the readership of the magazine. For some firms, this is the reason they are anxious to have articles appear with company affiliations noted; they wish to "promote" the products or concepts noted in the article. It can now be "merchandised." They capitalize on the credibility gained by having had the material appear in print, and may also capitalize on the prestige value, if any, of the magazine that published the article.

An article that appears in a publication lax in its standards has less post-publication value than one with a tough editor. It is at this point that the work demanded by the editor pays off. The author trades on the credibility and prestige value associated with the magazine and supplies something else of value to the editor—a publishable article—in order to make the exchange a more even one. The more highly the readers regard the publication, the greater the value of reprints and other merchandising activities related to the publication of the article.

PLEASE THE EDITOR, NOT YOUR PRESIDENT

Far too many corporate and consulting public relations personnel are placed in the untenable position of having to generate material for publication that meets the approval of corporate executives who have little or no comprehension of the role of a journal. These executives seem to try to use the business press for their narrow commercial purposes. This is often alien to the philosophy and mission of particular journals. Such executives may spend a large portion of their companies' funds for publicity purposes and may feel that the journals are a public service. Yet these executives would not attempt to make their product in a way that simply pleases their employees; they know they must please the consuming public.

Magazines are similarly constructed. A business or professional journal is not designed to please those who have news to tell; it is designed to please its readers. If it satisfies its readers, it will also satisfy its advertisers.

In addition to commercializing something that should not be presented in this manner, these same executives frequently demand that an author slant a submission to glamorize the top corporate personality. This makes the proposed article blatant press agentry—certainly not appropriate for publication in a prestigious journal.

When an article is proposed that must meet the desires of a corporate management which wishes to use a journal for its own selfish ends, the editor is left with only one option: reject the material outright. If corporate managers want publicity of this sort, as they may feel is their due, they can purchase advertising space to publish their messages. If they wish to gain credibility by having material appear in the editorial pages of a journal, they must conform to the morality of that journal. Anything less will bring almost certain refusal.

There are, to be sure, occasions when an article should be approved by the top corporate executives, particularly when such executives are to be quoted or the article concerns a proprietary development. It is not unusual for an article to be routed through the legal department or other departments before it is submitted to the editor, to assure that the facts and attitudes expressed actually reflect corporate policy.

This procedure represents an essential step in verifying factual data, and is respected—sometimes even demanded—by editors. Nevertheless, should the corporate legal department add "whereas"es, "and/or"s, and other legalese, the author may expect this material to be deleted or to have the otherwise acceptable article rejected at the last minute. Since most editors do not claim sufficient legal knowledge to know if their editing will change the legal sense, they will reject articles rather than subject their publications to possible lawsuits.

These are, of course, not the only areas of concern relating to company managements, but they are probably the greatest concerns to editors. The editor has the right to publish what he feels is appropriate and reject what he feels is inappropriate. No lawyer, company president, public relations executive, or other person outside his own publishing company can subsume that right for him or demand that privilege. What the editor does to mollify advertisers who demand this privilege will vary with the temperament and personality of each editor. A financial threat frequently leads to some moderation of the strongest position an editor would like to take; a complete surrender generally leads to a serious loss of prestige by the publication. It is seldom that a reputable advertiser will put such pressure on an editor.

Keep in mind that the editor is always going to have the final word on what appears in his magazine. This is his responsibility and his alone. It cannot be transferred or delegated. Even the publisher cannot absolve him of this responsibility. The publisher, who may pressure him to use certain material (especially if it has been submitted by or requested for submission by a major advertiser) cannot mandate publication. Yet, even here, the editor will use his prerogative to change style (if he wishes) and to question statements made by the author. Since the editor must answer for errors, assertions, and statements of purported fact that appear in his journal, he has the right to feel confident that he will not be pilloried for the errors of a contributor.

FOLLOW THE RULES, SEE THE RESULTS

There is no such thing as a guarantee of publication of any contributed article. Nevertheless, if you follow all the steps suggested in this book, you are likely to see your article reach print and to enjoy the personal benefits and satisfactions while your company or organization gains as well.

The more familiar you are with the procedures to follow, the more likely it is that you will be invited to submit material in the future when you query the editor about other ideas for articles. If the editor has been successful in his dealings with you, then you have been successful in your dealings with him. It is a transaction of mutual benefit.

Just because something has not been mentioned in this book is no reason to assume that you don't have to know it. Every editor has his own working style. He will ask you to meet his specific needs, not some generalized pattern described in this or any other book. If an editor wants you to do something you have not read about here, by all means follow his wishes. Your objective is to get your material published, not to make a point.

What follows represents a compilation of procedures and ideas that will usually work. If you apply these suggestions and are alert to the needs of particular editors, you will maximize the chance of getting your material into print.

NO GRAMMAR

It is not within the scope of this book to suggest what rules of grammar to use and how to put words onto paper. At no time in this volume will you see anything that refers to the "language arts." We can assume that if you can write an article, it will be in a language form that the editor can work with, even if it needs a lot of editing. The language of the article need not even be

English; the same general principles will apply regardless of the language used.

It will also be assumed that the writer knows his subject. Usually, the writer who is not adequately versed in his subject will not write well enough about it to get his article accepted. You are a professional, either a professional specialist or a professional writer. Either way, you know that a poorly researched and poorly documented article will not appeal to an editor whose reputation you stand to influence. Don't make any presumptions about what comprises documentation; if you are not certain, let the editor give you guidance.

Nowhere in this book will you find suggestions as to which writing style should prevail over which other writing style. Every editor has his own style and his own preferred method of presentation. Some like short, punchy sentences. Others like long expository statements and balanced sentences. A business or trade journal could use either. A professional or scientific journal also could use either, although there is a tendency for editors of these types of journals to tolerate longer and more complex grammatical constructions. If the journal is one that has an appeal to the academic community, a complex "academic" style will be acceptable in most instances and may even be preferred.

Good editors are somewhat flexible; their main objective is to correctly interpret the preferences of their readers. You don't even always have to write in the general style of the publication. Some editors like a variety of styles, especially with contributed material.

You may have read that only "good" writing can get published. This is begging the question because it presumes that published material is good writing. Much of what gets published is anything but good, as most people understand the term. Many articles that appear in the business press, and especially in professional journals, are turgid, ungrammatical, long-winded, and generally difficult to read. Because the term "good" is so subjective, and so susceptible to abuse, you won't find it used anywhere in this book. This book is not about the quality of writing; it is concerned only with the material's marketability.

DON'T ASSUME

We have done a lot of assuming in this introductory chapter. But there are certain assumptions you should be careful about making. Don't, for instance, assume that because a topic is of interest to you, the editor will agree. Don't assume that because the material is written well it will be considered publishable by any editor. Don't assume that because your work is definitive it will find an editor who will recognize its importance. And don't assume that you will be able to communicate better than the editor just because you write better and his grammar wouldn't even pass an elementary college course. Some editors are terrible writers but win awards because they are terrific communicators.

Just because you are aware of a particular topic that is coming to be of intense importance to your technology, specialty, or industry and represents a major step into the future, don't assume that the editor will welcome your material. Your timing may be off. You may be too early; you may be too late.

Don't take it for granted that because a topic is important to you and your industry, it will be important enough to appear in print and every editor in the field will know this. Some editors are not as smart as others. Some are smarter. You may lose out because an astute editor is aware that his readers, who are usually a large and diverse group, don't yet have enough background to read your article profitably. A less-than-astute editor may simply not know enough about what is happening to realize that your timing is correct and his is wrong.

If timing is your problem and the idea is sound, you have only to prolong your negotiations to make a convincing case, if a case can be made. Should you succeed, you will certainly see your work published, provided it meets all the other requisites of a suitable article.

MARKETING YOUR ARTICLE

When you put it all together, you will be making a product to order. You solicit a "customer," the editor. He tells you what his specifications for "purchasing" your product will be. You produce to these "specifications" or you don't make the "sale."

That is what this book is all about. As noted earlier, this is a book not about writing but about marketing—marketing your writing. When you have finished reading it, you will be able to refer to individual chapters for special procedures that you may need. Each chapter stands by itself as a smaller reference volume for each topic. This book itself represents a form of marketing. It is organized to market to you the information that the author, on the basis of his experience, believes is most important to writers in this field.

ATTITUDES OF HIGHER MANAGEMENT

Managements of companies and organizations are far more concerned with how their companies appear to their publics than they are with whether an article will sell products. In their view, the selling of products is taken care of by many structures within their organizations. The matter of image—the public affairs aspect—is a constant, all-consuming concern.

Image is important because it affects the total corporation. It affects the firm's ability to do business with customers, to generate capital, to find employees, to deal with government agencies on all levels. A good image is to be sought.

Articles that appear in the business and professional press are more likely to be matters affecting corporate image than matters of product sales. When managers speak of having "a good press," they are thinking at least partially of the business and professional press. They know articles can "sell" or "unsell" the company. They are aware of the influence of the business press in the money markets, in job markets, in professional areas, in government circles, and in many other areas of importance.

For this reason, management uses many techniques to generate articles on the one hand and to protect itself from questionable material on the other. Management may offer inducements to its own personnel, pay for professional personnel to write articles, and even try to "butter up" editors in a variety of honorable and not so honorable ways.

Management's interest in the business press is intense. An article that appears to reflect negatively on a company is enough to stimulate an active response from the top. Anything truly derogatory will certainly trigger a reaction.

In the pages that follow, you will see constant reminders of how aware editors in the business press are of the influential positions they possess in the business and professional world. They are cautious in wielding their power and careful with the editorial weight they can bring to bear against a business or industry. The business press is sometimes accused of being too mild with industry faults. But consider that an editor may have chosen this alternative over a less attractive one. Severity that damages is far more worthy of opprobrium than laxity that appears to condone. There is always time to build a stronger case, but it is hard to repair an unwarranted injury to a company's image.

You will see many examples of how editors work carefully, with extreme circumspection, to avoid publishing material that is incorrect, that can damage reputations needlessly, or that is in poor taste. You as an author will be expected to respect these editors and their judgments. Remember, an editor who is not respectful of his audience—all segments of his audience—will remain in his position only a very short time.

So, when you think of marketing your article, think of the overall circumstances surrounding your work, from initiation of idea through the entire process to final publication. You will be managing your article in the same way the editor manages his publication. You are the surrogate for the editor; you must understand the function you are undertaking. This book will show you how.

1

---

what is the
business press?

THERE ARE many different, and sometimes overlapping, defini-
tions of the terms "business press," "trade press," and "professional press." "Business" is the term that is broadest in scope; it
comprises all functions in which people earn their livings. For this
reason, the term "business press" will be used throughout this
book to refer to everything that is normally described as "trade
press," "professional journals," and, of course, "business press."
The older term "trade press" is the same as the newer term
"business press."

For our purposes, the business press will be viewed in terms of
editorial content and objectives. It comprises those publications
that are designed to be read by selected audiences whose occupational interests match the topics covered in the journal.

By using this definition, we can exclude those people who have
only a dilettante interest in a scientific, professional, or business
area and who do their primary business or professional work in
another field. Thus, we include managers, scientists, engineers,
technicians, doctors, lawyers, chemists, and insurance agents,
among many others. Magazines like *Business Week* and *Fortune*
are in the business press; one like *Scientific American* is not. This

is a special definition and is more useful only relative to writing for the appropriate journals. It is not a definition to be used for any other purposes.

In our definition, we have drawn no sharp distinction between business and professional publications. This is because some business magazines are very technical; some technical magazines are very commercial. The classification of business versus professional is too artificial for our purposes. If a magazine is in a field, it is designed to serve that field, whether you call that field an industry or a profession.

Certainly, the medical industry would prefer to call all of its facets professional, but the hospital administration portion of the medical field is truly an industry, not a profession. Medical practice is a profession, but a magazine that appeals to doctors because they are high-earning businesspeople is a business publication—or is it a consumer magazine?

The purpose here is not to determine what to call a publication but to convey how the writer can get his work published by the editor of that publication. Whatever the author wants to write about, there is someone out there to print it. There is also someone out there who is willing to read it, or at least read a good part of it.

An author who wishes to write for a particular group of readers in a specific industrial or commercial grouping will have to know which business and professional publications reach those readers. To mention the medical field again, some 500 different publications reach nurses, hospital administrators, doctors, interns, purchasing agents, therapists, and on and on and on. Should you wish to write about a particular prosthetic device, for instance, you need to know which medical practitioners would be most interested in knowing about it, and this may not be the group that seemed most logical at first thought.

In any "business" the best audience to try to reach may not be the group of people who will use a device but rather would be those who will recommend the use of it to others. This situation occurs in all industries. In most businesses, the users of equipment and services are seldom the people who authorize purchases of such equipment and services.

WHY DO PEOPLE READ BUSINESS PUBLICATIONS?

Why do people spend their time, often personal time, reading business publications? Why do they sometimes even prefer to receive their copies at home rather than in the office, plant, or laboratory? Why, indeed, should anyone spend his own or his company's money to pay for such magazines, when subscriptions must be paid for? Or, why should they indicate a willingness to receive other publications that are offered free to them as qualified readers?

The answer lies in the nature of the information provided by the business and professional press. The answer also lies in the reality that most people spend most of their lives at work, at their chosen occupations. And they want to keep improving themselves. Improvement generates income.

Certainly, anyone in a business or profession can learn of new developments by researching the formal literature in the field. Sooner or later—generally sooner—he or she will find that the business press comprises much of the formal and cataloged literature. This is in addition to carrying news of an industry or profession on a regular basis. The answer, when all is said and done, is that the business and professional press provides information of value that cannot be obtained anywhere else or in as rapid and timely a fashion. Each publication is a vehicle that has been devised in response to the needs of the people in the industry it serves.

Thus, a primary function of the professional press and of some business publications is to report on new developments, new concepts, or new approaches to existing practices. The press researches news that its editors feel will be of interest to or of value to the readers. The long articles, which are the major editorial product, are geared to inform the reader of developments in an objective way.

A second major function of the business press is to offer interpretations and opinions that will make the readers better informed. Only the business press can offer an overview and still remain impartial vis-à-vis technical developments. It can place important new developments in a perspective that interested individuals cannot perceive because of their partisanship or closeness to the unfolding circumstances. In short, it offers balance.

A third major function is to publish details of developments that are still proprietary or in an evolutionary stage. When the editor and his informants have established a good rapport and mutual trust, this can be done without compromising the sources while, at the same time, advancing the interests of the industry, business, or profession.

A fourth major function is to offer instructional material and information for readers. The how-to article is a very basic type of piece (and will be described in Chapter 6). How-to articles provide information that enables an industry or profession to compete more effectively with another industry or profession or that provides interpretations of existing or new requirements. An accounting publication, for example, can instruct accountants in how to interpret new tax laws by having experts write for the publication, either on staff or by invitation. A medical publication can go through a step-by-step procedure for implanting a new type of artificial organ. A general business journal can instruct its readers in the pitfalls of new liability regulations and what they entail in personnel and legal requirements.

News is important too. Presentation of news of current industry or professional activity is a major function of many publications and may comprise a large percentage of the editorial product. Such news may include information about new products; literature available free or for a fee; changes in titles and organizational affiliations of industry personnel; information about corporate or organization activities, changes, and moves; news of new books and reviews of books and other major specialized publications; financial information; and other special information in various "columns" as may suit the marketplace served by the journal.

VERTICAL/HORIZONTAL/FUNCTIONAL

Business journals have generally been classified as either vertical or horizontal. A vertical publication is one that attempts to cover all facets of an entire integrated industry. That is, it publishes news of the industry relating to anything from raw materials through marketing. The magazine *Iron Age* was one such magazine in its heyday. It served the steel industry in all its facets, up to and including management and marketing of the products. It was not concerned with the technology of the industry except insofar as this technology was reflected in the marketing by the industry. It left to metallurgical publications the matter of technology. It still does.

Horizontal publications offer material that is primarily of interest to a very large group of specialists who work in a large number of different industries. A magazine such as *Instruments and Control Systems* will have readers in the glass industry as well as those who work for railroads, for airlines, or in candy factories. The orientation is toward the exposition of the details of a technology, not necessarily toward its narrow application in a specific industrial setting. New product publications are also examples of such broadly focused magazines.

I have added a third classification of business journals: diagonal. A diagonal journal is one that conveys information and adopts an editorial policy that cuts across the combination of both vertical and horizontal.

The publications that I call diagonal are sometimes referred to as "phenomenon-oriented" or "function-oriented." These are publications concerned with what happens when a particular technology is applied within a limited industrial, commercial, technical, or scientific environment.

Materials handling publications, for example, generally fall within this classification. There are specialists in this technology, but they may work either within vertical spheres, such as in the industry that transports and forwards products, or in companies that have to move products around in order to conduct their main business.

Some magazines that appear to be vertical or horizontal may actually be functional. An author who wishes to reach an audience for such a journal has a more difficult task analyzing reader interest than he would for either a true vertical or a true horizontal publication. As a rule, the outstanding, most widely read, and most highly regarded magazines in any "vertical" field are really those which are phenomenon-oriented, and their editorial demands are far more stringent than are those of any other types of business publications.

The true vertical magazine was born in the middle of the last century, serving a particular industry as the Industrial Revolution created true industries. Vertical magazines arose first in the United States, where centralized communications were impossible to establish—as could be done easily in European countries with central cities. Initially, many of these journals were little more than gossipy sheets, telling their readers, who were widely dispersed geographically, things they could not learn except by constant attention to the minutiae of industry activities. The editor collected details from all over through correspondence, and returned the favor by publishing them all in one place.

Horizontal publications began to become important when, in the latter decades of the nineteenth century, the Industrial Revolution spread to large segments of commercial life. Too much technology had created a separate class of specialists whose talents were equally at home in one or another industry, but whose interests were not limited by the functions of the industry. Many horizontal journals were first published by the professional societies that were being formed rapidly to cope with the explosion of new technical data.

The phenomenon-oriented publications began to make their mark in the 1920s. A vast amount of specialized information was becoming available to technologists working in specialized areas with the broadest range of industrial applications. Magazines covering applications of materials, technologies, and talents were developed to meet these individual needs. A large subgroup of such publications might alternatively be called "applications-oriented," except that some of the professional publications which fall logically into this classification are not concerned with application of technology but solely with the exposition of data sufficient for astute readers to develop their own applications.

This type of publication is especially useful in industrial situations that involve highly sophisticated technology. For instance, when a company employs an entire computer department, the members of that department must know their computer technology as well as the business of the company and how the technology can be applied in the industrial setting.

More recently, a large number of publications have found excellent reader acceptance by converting their vertical or horizontal approaches into "functional" ones. This development became quite marked following World War II. It occurred because many engineers and scientists are expected by their employers to have at least an awareness, if not a detailed knowledge, of the economics involved in implementing scientific and technological developments. These technical personnel are frequently the ones who specify products and processes. Since many managers have risen through the engineering route, they are capable of understanding newer approaches to technology.

TECHNICAL/MANAGEMENT/NEWSY?

Which approach does an editor prefer? If you are going to write for a magazine, you should know what the editor is likely to want you to produce.

If the magazine has a technical orientation, don't send it a folksy article. If it serves management, don't send it a detailed technical exposition because it won't be read by most managers. If its approach is that of a weekly or monthly newsmagazine, it would not pay to submit a long article. In short, whether the magazine uses any of these approaches or some other one, the person who wishes to have something published should know what type of material is most likely to get a reading, and possibly publication.

HOW LARGE IS THE BUSINESS PRESS?

Some 10 years ago, someone made a good estimate that the business and professional press included over 3,000 different publications. Those publications which are owned and published by professional organizations and associations for the exclusive use of their members were excluded from the total. Yet, at that time, the estimate was also made that in the United States alone the business press was growing at a compound rate of 10 percent per year.

This would imply that there are now more than 6,000 different business and professional publications that have some commercial orientation, at least in part. Some will accept only limited amounts and types of advertising, as for example those professional publications which accept advertising only for books. Some will accept any advertising offered.

The number of people employed directly by the business press has been estimated at about 50,000 editorial, plus at least twice that number in sales, production, and clerical positions. It is not a large number by most industry standards.

Advertising supports the business press. Advertising revenue has been reliably reported at about $2 billion, not nearly approaching that of daily newspapers or the television industry. Actual revenues can never really be known because of major revenue-producing publications that are sometimes classified in one category and then another. At times a publication is classified both as a consumer and as a business publication. One such example is *Forbes*. The classification may depend more on where the advertising comes from than on the readers to whom the magazine is distributed.

HOW DEEP DOES THE BUSINESS PRESS PENETRATE?

Today, when a technology is just emerging, it is almost immediately served by a newsletter. Since newsletters can become financially viable with but a few hundred or fewer subscribers, this is the easiest way for the press to penetrate a field.

Sometimes a professional group will set up a special editorial department in an established journal for an emerging specialty developing in its area. This later gets spun off to become a separate entity with its own very large audience.

When any major activity becomes important—as, for example, environmental or occupational health issues resulting from legislative or public action—magazines spring up like weeds after a spring rain. Like weeds, as soon as the weather turns unfavorable, they wither. But some always seem to survive, and they become the nucleus of a group of magazines that serves the emerging industry.

It is almost axiomatic that a business or industry will have a business or professional publication, or both, within a few years after it is identified and recognized.

FREQUENCY OF PUBLICATION

The business press publishes anywhere from daily, as in the case of *Women's Wear Daily* and some legal newspapers, to annually. Some publications come out even less frequently than this. Some are published irregularly—by design, not by financial necessity. There are semi-weeklies, tri-weeklies, weeklies, bi-weeklies, fortnightlies, semi-monthlies, monthlies, bi-monthlies, quarterlies, and semi-annuals. Annuals tend to be confined very largely to directories, as do many of the semi-annuals.

Your best market when trying to get your articles published is in the monthlies; there are just so many more of them than all the others combined. Your poorest market is with the dailies, which are newspapers in every sense of the word except that they have specialized audiences. There is no market whatsoever in annuals, unless they carry some special editorial material, such as the twelfth issue of *Modern Packaging*, which was partially encyclopedic in nature. Contributions to such special issues are usually by invitation.

In one sense, preparation of editorial matter in the business press is unlike that in newspapers, where everything reported on is current and has occurred within a very short span of time prior to publication. On the other hand, preparation of editorial matter in the business press is similar to that in newspapers because both have columnists, special "backgrounders" (reports that bring current developments up to date with a historical perspective), "departments," and the like.

The business press works well in advance of publication date to develop good "story" material. This offers contributors a chance to get something published. The dailies, like general newspapers, are not likely to take very much that you can supply and put your name on. If your material purports to be news, they may accept it but they will check it out carefully and then write their own version. If it is opinion, your name will be used because this tends to show readers that any statements you make are attributable to a contributor, generally assumed to be a reader, rather than to the journal.

The same is true of magazines such as *Business Week*, which operates on a very short turnaround schedule. Nevertheless, this magazine does print in-depth articles and publishes contributed material if that material is timely.

The meaning of timeliness may vary with the journal. What seems timely to a sophisticated industry may be premature for general business. This factor enables contributing editors to penetrate the latter markets. They actually may have weeks or months to work on an article. When the article is finally published, it will be timely.

Each journal has its own method that has enabled it to prosper. If a magazine is the only one in a small industry it may well be able to get away with publishing material that is months old. If it is one of many in a highly competitive, large industry, it will find its niche in specialization. This may keep an editor from over-working the editorial staff to keep the material timely.

Each magazine is different. Each has its own personality. Each one that you may want to write for has to be approached individually. When doing so, you will be expected to respect the time frame requirements. Don't presuppose that all magazines with the same frequency of issuance operate on the same lead time before publication.

When you make your queries, you will find out just what the magazine editor wants. Some editors will be easier to work with than others. Some will be more lax concerning time for delivery of your article and the timeliness of your material. You will just have to find out what is needed.

COMPANY MAGAZINES

Some people would classify company magazines, or house organs, as business or professional journals. That they are, but they differ from commercial publications in that even when articles are not written by staff personnel of the journals them-selves, they are written by employees of the companies that publish the journals. As a result, the special research, art, photography, and other nonwriting functions, as well as the requirements for acceptance of articles, are quite different from those of independent publications.

One major difference is that the approval process for under-taking a writing project is different. Many articles are written by direction rather than by choice of the author. Further, there is usually a looser set of standards for the writing style because more editorial assistance is given. There are also differences in the commitment to deadlines, which can be enforced by the company executives; in the amount and type of editorial support provided; and more.

Because there are so many and such significant differences between company magazines and independent journals, there is no special mention of company magazines in this book. However, circumstances may exist in which the approach to a company magazine is very similar to that which would be taken toward a publication supported by advertising or a publication of a professional society. When such similarities exist, the ideas and recommendations given in the chapters that follow may prove helpful. If they do, so much the better.

Company magazines cannot be pigeonholed into classifications very easily, any more than business and professional journals can be classified easily. They vary all over the lot. Unless you are already familiar with a particular company magazine that you want to write for, you will have to go through a process of selection that is not unlike what you would do for independent journals. The number of company magazines is legion. Most are not open to outside contributions, except by invitation.

2

---

who reads business and professional magazines?

IF YOU WANT to reach an audience of any sort, you have to know who they are and where they are. You must identify the components of your most desirable audience and locate the readers.

Every business or professional journal has a special audience that it has catered to for some time. It directs its entire editorial package to that specific audience. Although at first glance it may appear that the audience is quite diverse, you will always find a common denominator with any successful journal.

As an example, some magazines target their articles to management within an industry. Others specialize in production. Still others are heavily involved in application of technology, emphasizing how things are done. And some concentrate on highly sophisticated and advanced theoretical scientific thinking.

In seeking to divide these "markets" you might think in terms of the five "W"s and the "H" of the famous Abbott and Costello comedy routine. It is almost as complex to figure out who is on first and what is on second in the business and professional press as it was in that outstanding comedy act.

WHO'S ON FIRST?

Let's start out with the "who."

Some magazines find that their primary audience comprises individuals who are interested mostly in news about people: their movement, their changes in job positions and company affiliations. It is not unlike the high school newsletter sent to alumni telling where classmates are now, whom they have married, and what jobs they have. People like to know about people; most of us have a taste for gossip.

You must look deeply to establish that this is a primary audience. It is not easy because in order to leaven the published product a magazine will include other material as well. You can easily be misled. As a general rule, magazines that have a regional or local appeal tend to emphasize people, the "who" of the five "W"s.

WHAT OF THE "WHAT"?

The next of our "W"s is "what."

This is a bit easier to identify. Primary examples of magazines that subscribe to this philosophy are the new product journals. They abound in every field, from electronics to school supplies, from nuclear products to packaging. Many of them use a tabloid format. All have reader-service, or "bingo," cards, with numbers that enable readers to respond to both editorial and advertised items.

New product publications carry advertising as well as general editorial items. They frequently have a relatively rigid format, particularly if they carry only information on new products and new literature. Almost none carry news about people or about the industry in general. A few of these publications carry general news or interpretive articles as well. However, there is generally little or no interpretation of the news items carried, only factual and technical data. These journals are, in effect, short-form catalogs. The reader selects from them the items in which he is interested, circles the appropriate reader-service number on the bingo card, and then receives a detailed data sheet or catalog (or salesperson) from the maker or seller.

Readers of these magazines get their information quickly and in a distilled, almost sterile form. Such magazines are designed to be read, annotated, and discarded quickly. The news in such journals pales very quickly. They function as little more than newsletters for their readers, and tend to be just about as invaluable.

Nevertheless, the popularity of these magazines can be attested to by their immense circulations—usually free to qualified readers. In most industries, these magazines have the largest circulation of any of the publications serving the industry.

"WHERE" IS NEXT

A surprising amount of major editorial space is devoted to telling readers where things are happening. Few journals specialize in publishing this type of information, but it is a very important feature for most readers.

Given information that something is taking place within his industry, the reader wants to know where it is happening in order to believe what is written. This points up the importance of establishing credibility when you write your article, and stating where an action has occurred is important to that end.

The truly vertical publication, which is becoming increasingly rare, is a magazine that specializes in telling readers where things are happening, where they will probably happen, and where they will certainly happen. In the preceding chapter we discussed the emergence of the vertical magazine concept as one which brought together news from many geographical locations. Such journals were publishing news of events that were occurring in locations distant from the readers, but that were of interest to them.

The true vertical publication has been almost completely transformed into a more general news publication. Many of the journals that did not make this transition have been supplanted by ones that did. Such publications now carry all types of articles, some of them very technical, some oriented toward management, others aimed at production personnel. It is possible to spread the editorial coverage in this manner because the readers will respond favorably, having been conditioned over many years to receive information and news in this fashion.

Articles published in a journal with a "where" orientation are not necessarily short, although this tends to be a pattern that has worked for them. Long articles, prepared by either staff or contributors, are frequently collations of available data concerning something of reader interest. Roundup articles are commonplace here. Such articles tend to have a strong "where" flavor.

"WHEN" IS TIMELINESS

When is the "when" approach most found? It is appropriate to the newspaper-like dailies and high-frequency publications. The reader is approaching the news with a major concern for its timeliness. He knows he must act upon what he reads, if he does act upon it, within a short period of time following publication of the information.

Even though a reader may have a primary and overriding interest in timeliness, he frequently welcomes published material that falls into another "W" class. Each of the "when"-oriented journals publishes other news of its industry likely to interest people in the field.

Some journals that publish with less frequency than dailies or weeklies include material that seems timely, but obvious limitations are imposed by their production cycles. The concept of timeliness is different for each journal. If a monthly magazine needs a minimum of a full month to produce any given article, it is certainly unlikely to be able to be first to disclose news about legislation; this will probably have been published weeks earlier somewhere else. It can, and does, publish interpretations of the legislation, while the "when"-oriented magazine publishes the facts of the legislation. Therein lie the importance and circumscription of the "when"-oriented journals.

"WHY" IS PERTINENT

If you want to write to management, you want to get your article into a magazine that takes the "why" point of view. Managers cannot act without understanding the justifications for their actions. You have to tell a management reader why a given action on his part is justifiable.

If you want to write to the marketing people in an industry, you also will try to publish in a magazine of this sort. Further, it is the type of journal to use when you want to reach technical people who have high-level financial responsibilities.

All three groups are in positions where actions that they take or propose must be justified to stockholders, boards of directors, presidents, and other high-level corporate officials. They need facts but, more important, they need reasons for their actions.

All three groups are responsible for financial matters that affect their companies. Although it may not seem that a corporate technical director is a financial figure in his company, think of the havoc he could raise by authorizing that money be spent in a fruitless research and development venture rather than in one that will lead to new business.

If you look carefully at the most successful business journals and at many of the better professional journals, you will see that the "why" approach predominates. These magazines are neither horizontal (as the "what" magazines) nor vertical (as the "where" journals). They are the phenomenon- or function-oriented magazines when they are technical; they are similarly oriented when they are directed exclusively to management.

It is not always easy to see this in a magazine. A tipoff that a journal is "why"-directed can be found in the concept of the "bottom line." If many articles in a magazine provide data that enable decisions to be made that affect profitability, the magazine has a bottom-line orientation.

An article in a "why" journal may look like any other article in any other magazine, but it differs in that it always includes an implied or explicit financial justification. This is true whether the story is about a plant installation, a new technology, a marketing opportunity, a change in dealing with personnel, matters of occupational health and safety, product liability, product development, or what have you. If you write for such a journal you must answer the reader's question: "What's in it for me?" If you cannot, or will not, answer that question, your article would probably not be accepted by a magazine of this sort.

HOW TO REACH THE "HOW" MARKET

By far the largest number of business magazines are in the area of "how." Maybe it is because readers are so interested in "What's in it for me" that they look for information that will help them do their jobs better.

More people are doing work than are directing work. This is the thrust of the "how" journals. Unfortunately for publishers, this group reads magazines much less frequently than the decision-makers—the managers—the group that is most concerned with when and why. Many publishers of "how" journals stress their large readership. They will "prove" to an advertiser that he can get more reader-service inquiries from this type of magazine than from any other except the new product journals. And they are right. But the people who make decisions often do not respond to cards; they use the telephone. Or, they have others do the responding for them.

Articles in "how"-oriented magazines are truly instructional, sometimes reading almost like technical manuals. In industries that are served by a very large number of journals, such as the electronics, computer, and chemicals fields, there are specialized journals that provide only this type of information. But most journals that emphasize this approach also publish other types of articles.

Magazines in this category also tend to be function-oriented.

Since our modern society and industries are so complex, it is rare to find an event that does not impinge on other circumstances. It can be assumed that the reader knows something that is central to his specialty but also realizes he needs skills and knowledge from other specialties. Article content covers this range. Contributed materials are extremely welcome to meet this need.

A contributor can normally supply the crossover technology that the staff writers often lack. If some 20 different related technologies impinge on a specialty, it is unlikely that the staff writers can all be sufficiently knowledgeable to write intelligently about all of them. Contributors can.

As an example, if we were to consider the materials forwarding and handling industry, we would find that it involves, among other specialties, all of the following: packaging, computers, data retrieval, product retrieval, printing, electronic sensing, truck and rail regulations, interstate transport laws, the intrastate laws of 50 states, international lading rules, meteorology (yes, weather is important), refrigeration and heating, and ocean currents. If you are proposing an article for a journal in the materials handling industry, you often must be able to give information on all the appropriate ancillary specialties related to your main topic.

PROFILING AN AUDIENCE

If you want to sell a product, you have to know who is willing to buy it and why. If you want to get an article published, you have to direct it to those who would want to read it. In other words, you have to know who you want to reach and how to define members of this group. You go about finding this out in the same way a company goes about formulating its advertising and promotion program.

To formulate an advertising program, you first decide what market—what people in a given group—you want to reach. Then you formulate a specific set of plans for reaching that group. Actually, public relations experts tend to have a clearer picture of the business and professional press than advertising people do. This is because they are not influenced by the numbers of people that a magazine reaches; they are more concerned with the value of the readers to their clients and of the readers' influence. They would rather have an article appear in a journal that reaches the precise audience they want than have the same article appear in a much more widely circulated journal with a smaller group of influential readers.

The professional public relations executive may be concerned not only with the suitability of an article's contents for a particular journal but with his ability to exploit the appearance of the article in the journal. The mere appearance of an article in a publication will not suffice; there may be an ulterior public relations objective. Just as space advertising is designed to meet a marketing objective, public relations has objectives. Many of them are far more complex than advertising people may think.

Many technical journals and industry publications are read by small groups of very influential people, such as Wall Street analysts. Although the major thrust of an article may well appear to be technological, a not inconsiderable value is that of reaching the few "influentials" who are also readers. Public relations professionals are frequently even more aware of this secondary audience than the editors.

Future merchandising value could be another objective. If an article about a company or organization appears in an especially prestigious journal, perhaps one with a very limited circulation, the future merchandising value may be tremendous. Merely to have written an article that could pass the stringent requirements of a review board for the journal may imply the highest level of acceptability in that industry. Reprinting of the article by the thousands would provide far greater circulation than the readership of the journal that carried the article.

Another reason public relations specialists have a clearer picture is that they specialize in dealing with the print media. Advertising people have more media to consider and cannot learn enough about all of them. They really never get to know the print media intimately unless they are specialists in this area. This is not to their discredit, but an author should watch carefully that he does not follow one line of reasoning when the other is more appropriate. Your own requirements as an author may call for one or the other; neither is to be automatically preferred.

PLAN THE DEMOGRAPHICS

To profile an audience, consider the demographics. This is the basis of all advertising. Study of this subject will serve you well in selecting a group of journals as likely prospects for your articles. The term "demographics" is being used here in the broadest sense only. We are not really concerned with income levels but with decision-making levels, so our discussion of demographics will revolve around that approach.

Each article will have a desired objective. If you don't clearly define your objective, your article may meander. Think in terms of your objective and you will automatically think in terms of the reader. Now you have to define that reader—give him characteristics.

Take your desired reader and define him in terms of some of the following characteristics. Don't confine yourself to this list, which is only a guide. You will have some special interests that pertain only to your own work.

Managerial responsibilities
Technical responsibilities
Production responsibilities
Quality assurance responsibilities
Education and learning
Literacy level
Training
Responsibility for profit and loss
Responsibility for directing others

Responsibility for such areas as research, development, re-
search *and* development, sales, marketing, and sales man-
agement
Academic level of achievement
Budgetary restraints
Ability to commit funds above or below a given amount
Requirement to consult others before committing funds over a
certain limit
Academic duties

If you have to write to a high school academic achievement
level, you want to avoid terms and sentence structures that
would be grasped readily only by Ph.D.s. If you have to reach
members of boards of directors, you need to be aware of the
limits on their time and must make sure your writing can be read
quickly and comprehended unambiguously.

When you have profiled your desired reader, you will have
done more than predetermine the journal to select; you will also
have created a set of conditions for your writing style. As an
example, I have profiled my audience for this book as primarily
college graduates who have specialized knowledge in a particular
technology. I have also included those who have writing skills
and the ability to research material that has a technical content of
some complexity. That is, they have the ability to learn enough
about the technology in question to enable them to write intelligently about it.

In writing to my reader, I know that he (or she) can read and
understand a long sentence, appreciates a short sentence, and
does not want to read jumpy copy. So, I modify my writing
appropriately.

I have also selected the market for this book. My publisher has
identified the markets that this book can be sold to and also
identified some markets that cannot be reached directly without
excessive effort or expense. So, we only hope that these latter
markets will find us.

You will be doing much the same thing with your article. You have to identify your audience before you even propose an article to an editor. If you propose an idea to an editor and he accepts it, but you have identified your reader incorrectly, you are likely to find a rejection upon submission of your article. You will have done everything right, but for another journal. You won't know it because you have put last things first.

Your goal in marketing your "product," your article, is to reach the market for it through the medium of the editor and his journal. If you identify that market correctly, you will succeed; if you do not, you will fail. It is just as simple as that.

DEFINE THE READER'S CHARACTERISTICS

The first steps, as we have seen, are to plan your article to match the audience you believe wants to read it and to roughly identify your audience by profiling it. The next step is to write down the most important characteristics that you feel define your desired audience, in order of decreasing importance.

Start your list with the most important features of the reader, then proceed to the lesser, more expendable characteristics. As an example, if you are writing to paper technologists, you might instinctively feel your article or paper should appear in *TAPPI* magazine. But what if your article or paper is not about research but is about development? You may find that this would not be the most appropriate journal to publish your paper in. Also, although your article concerns a new development in paper, it may be that one segment of this industry is better represented by a business magazine than by a professional one. Which magazine do you try to get into?

If you profile your audience, you might come up with something like this:

Primary:
1. Paper physicists and technologists
2. Linerboard (corrugated container) specialists
3. Individuals with a Ph.D. or M.S. degree

4. People with engineering and application responsibilities
5. People who work in the industry.

Secondary:

1. Managers who need this information in order to implement changes
2. People knowledgeable about packaging applications
3. People who work in paper mills
4. People who work in converting plants
5. People who direct follow-up work

With a profile of this sort you can establish that you do not want to publish in *TAPPI*, the professional journal of the Technical Association of the Pulp & Paper Industry. *TAPPI* does not reach people who are involved in the engineering applications of linerboard but only those who are involved in basic research in this technology. A better choice is the business journal *Paperboard Packaging*, which is phenomenon-oriented, covers the linerboard application industry, reaches virtually all paper physicists and technologists in this specialty, and reaches nearly all those in the industry who have engineering and application responsibilities. The difference between the two journals shows up in item 2 in the list of the primary characteristics. The business journal is able to reach more of these individuals than the professional journal.

Having defined and refined your audience profile, you would now approach the editor of *Paperboard Packaging*. In preparing the article, you would tailor your writing to the particular audience you have defined. This does not mean that the remainder of the magazine will be written in that style. Far from it. Your sentences will be longer than sentences in articles about machinery. Your graphics will be more complex than those depicting business trends in the industry. You have profiled and selected your audience; the editor knows that his magazine reaches this audience. He will not be fearful that your writing will appeal only to a high academic level. Rather, he will welcome your paper because it gives him a chance to show that his magazine appeals to this group.

DON'T WRITE DOWN TO THE READER

Having defined your audience, having defined the publication that you prefer, and having established the ability of your audience to comprehend your material, both technically and academically, you have established your proper writing niche. Now stick to it.

There is a great temptation to try to make your article appeal to all levels of readers in a magazine. Don't. If you dilute your technology, you will lose your most valued group of readers. If you dilute your writing style, you will also lose them.

If you don't dilute either, you will probably gain many readers who you hadn't thought would comprehend what you are writing about. Since you have preselected a high-level group, the less knowledgeable readers will be complimented that you have chosen to expose your ideas in a magazine that they read.

The famous story about the taxi driver who said he could understand the speeches of the late Adlai Stevenson but he did not think the average citizen could, should tell you something about your audience. You may think many readers won't be able to understand you, but they will. Believe in their potential. You would be surprised at the value a less informed, less educated reader can extract from an article when the contents concern him, even indirectly or marginally.

If you have a simple story to tell, make it simple and straightforward. Use technical terms if you have to, however. Don't assume that because you use some technical terms the person working at a fairly low level in the industry will not understand them. Policemen understand the wording and meaning of the laws they enforce, even though they are not attorneys. Industry personnel know their terms and terminology also.

WHAT ARE THE INTERESTS OF READERS?

What are readers interested in?

Me! Me! Me!

Yes, readers are like all of us. They are interested in themselves more than in anything else, more than in anyone else.

You are reading this book because you can get something of value from it that will enable you to do your work better, will make you feel better, and, perhaps most important, will make you appear better and more important in the eyes of your colleagues, friends, and family. This appeals to all of us. If I were to write about my experiences as an editor, you would be bored to tears—or more likely, would put down this book before you got past page 3. A person's self-interest will determine what he chooses to read, including items to help him do his job better.

Sometimes the desire for self-importance can lead to excesses affecting distribution of journals. In one high-technology aerospace company, the electronics engineers all tried to receive as many journals and catalogs as they could and to get their names on as many professional mailing lists as possible. It seems that prestige in that section depended on how high the pile of mail was on each engineer's desk each morning.

Everyone wants and needs a pat on the back, needs to feel important. The business and professional journals cater, even if the editors don't consciously verbalize this, to the reader who wants to improve himself, to become more important. The average reader thinks of himself as someone who has special access to information because he reads a particular business or professional journal. He views himself as someone special. He sees this as offering him an opportunity to prove his own view of himself.

The businessman wants to do a better job so he can earn more money. If he is an entrepreneur, he relishes the prestige he gets within his community as an employer of heads of families, a bringer of wealth to the community. If he is a manager, he dotes on the praise given him when the board of directors tells him that his work is excellent. When his company does well and the stockholders are pleased, he receives compliments in front of his most important constituency.

If he is a middle-level executive, he enjoys the approbation of his higher-level corporate officers who tell him what a good job he has done. He might have picked up some ideas from your article.

If he is a technical manager and he introduces an improvement or a new idea, he is complimented by a promotion, a raise, or just the praise he gets when he has helped his organization do its appointed task better than a competitor.

If he is a professional practitioner, he enjoys knowing that he has solved a problem that was disturbing him. He also knows that his reputation is based on the word that clients send out concerning his excellence and skills, be he lawyer, doctor, accountant, or plumber.

If he is a machine operator and picks up some ideas from a magazine, he turns out more or better work. It gets noticed first by his fellow workers and then by his management. Rewards follow.

If he is an academician, his love of learning is usually accompanied by a love of praise. When he reads of a new idea, he can use it as a citation in a paper. And because of his ability to keep up with the most arcane aspects of his field he is rewarded by having his own paper accepted to be read at professional meetings.

Now let us relate this to the business and professional press.

IF READERS SPEND TIME AND MONEY, WHY?

Where can all these people get the greatest amount of knowledge in the least amount of time with the least effort? They can get it from the business and professional press—and only there. It comes to them in a distilled form, ready for consumption. It comes already packaged in a form that enables direct extraction of ideas. This is the service the business and professional press provides. This is why people will read, why they will spend their personal time boning up on a business or technology, why they sometimes spend their own money to buy such magazines. Companies and organizations buy such publications for the very same reasons. Companies and organizations comprise people, and they want to keep those people well informed.

Information of value doesn't always come from top-quality sources. Of what value is a second-rate journal to a subscriber? The answer was given by one such subscriber who told me: "If we get one good idea in a year, we have repaid our subscription price."

In most fields, it is not possible for any one journal to cover all the developments that readers are interested in. The "market" for several journals is created and assured by this condition. The journals divide up the field; they specialize. One will concentrate on the "what" approach, one on the "why" concept, and so forth. Each has something to offer its readers.

READERS WEAR MANY HATS

Given the diversity of journals in a narrow field, how do readers tend to view their magazines? If two magazines have differing points of view but tend to publish similar material, what is it that distinguishes them?

The answer lies in the attitudes of the readers when they read their journals. Readers have expectations about what they will derive from each journal they read. In effect, they wear different occupational and intellectual hats when they read different journals.

A manager who is responsible for production and for technology developments will read two magazines, one specializing in production problems and solutions, the other in technology development. Both will carry articles that overlap into the other's primary field. When reading one journal, however, the manager will tend not to really see the articles that he feels "belong" to the other. He is reading in accordance with his expectations.

When you plan to approach editors of such journals with your article idea, your best opportunity will lie in knowing which type of article belongs most appropriately in which type of journal. But you must also consider another factor. If you think you are more likely to be able to place your article with the magazine that specializes in the area you have covered, think again. Think carefully. Won't this magazine receive many more solicitations from authors who propose to write articles of this sort than the magazine for which the subject is marginal? Also, the specialized magazine generally has staff personnel who write on the specialty and may not accept as many contributed articles.

The other magazine doesn't get many solicitations for articles of this sort. Its staff is not skilled in this area. You are more likely to get a favorable reception here, and much more likely to see early publication.

But, do you really want this? If you want to obtain the best value subsequent to publication—the merchandising value— strive to get into the journal that specializes in your area.

In some industries, the differences between magazines may not be very great. In others, the differences may be dramatic. You must find out how the readers view the magazines and conduct yourself accordingly. You will be well repaid for your efforts.

3

---

know the publications you are interested in

YOU HAVE AN IDEA for an article. You feel for certain that there are people out in the unknown who are going to be interested in what you have to say. Or, you are certain that your material will interest some editor in your chosen field. You are sure of your material. How do you find the right journal? Where do you look to see which journals reach the field?

You may know the magazine in a particular field because you are an active participant in that industry. You may know some and prefer to see your material only in those because you favor them and believe that your judgment is sound—and it probably is. You may have had some experience with a group of publications in an industry and have already rated them. You may know some of the editors quite well from previous associations and can even ask one of them with whom you are quite friendly to make a recommendation. If any of the foregoing is true, then you will have little or no problem deciding how and where to try to place an article.

But what if you don't know where to turn? What if your experience has been narrow, albeit deep, in a field and now you have to go, for instance, from a technology orientation to an application area? Are there some published sources that can help you?

The answer is a definite yes. On second thought, maybe it should be a tentative yes, because you still have no means by which to compare the suitability of various journals for your requirements. You would have had to live with them to really know them well.

REFERENCE SOURCES

One of the most popular sources for finding good outlets for articles is one that is not even designed for this purpose. It is the guidebook most used by advertising agencies, published by Standard Rate and Data Service. The guidebook lists both business publications and other media. The volume for you to use is "Business Rates and Data," published bi-monthly. You need not work with the latest edition; changes are not frequent or drastic, so a volume up to a year old would still be quite useful.

These listings are neither complete nor definitive; they are not intended to be. But they are incredibly good, depending on what you are looking for. If you are looking for those industry magazines that accept advertising, *SRDS* is the only truly competent source to work with. It carries information about such things as circulation, advertising rates, market served, and demographic and geographic editions published. (You may be interested in this information if you have a story of limited interest. Such an article might be more suited to one of these limited-circulation editions than to the full run.)

SRDS is limited in that it excludes many publications which are not audited, that is, verified by an independent auditing agency. An audit usually means that the journal actually has the circulation it claims. Unaudited publications may or may not provide correct figures.

If a publication does not choose to have a listing in *SRDS*, it simply refuses to be listed. There are some excellent journals that carry advertising yet are not listed, by their own choice.

The volume that lists business and trade publications includes those published in the United States, plus a smattering of some published elsewhere in the world, except Canada. There is a separate volume for Canadian journals. As a first cut, refer to *SRDS* for information about the journals you may want to consider for articles. Virtually all the major business publications are listed.

Only the very largest public libraries carry this reference book. You will find it, however, in all advertising agencies that have industrial accounts, as well as in the advertising departments of most large business concerns. If you do not have access to the latest edition, a friend at an advertising agency may be able to get an older copy that is being discarded.

PUBLIC RELATIONS GUIDES

A number of clipping services publish public relations guides. The best known is *Bacon's Publicity Checker*, published by Bacon's Publishing Company. It is available for a price and gives, in brief form, some of the same data as are carried in *SRDS*. In addition, *Bacon's* will tell you whether the journal publishes various types of press releases, uses editorial illustrations, charges for artwork, and more. This guide has somewhat broader classifications than SRDS, yielding more journals per classification and sometimes joining two apparently dissimilar industrial classifications under a single heading.

The listings are free to publications and are verified periodically. Unfortunately, too many editors who receive the updating forms do not take the trouble to make corrections and changes. As a result, some of the data carried in *Bacon's* are obsolete. This is unfortunate and can result in problems for you unless you check out the information with the editors directly.

Other guides include published journals that cater to free-lance writers, such as *The Writer* and *Writer's Markets*. These guides vary in reliability but are certainly at least as reliable as *Bacon's*. The information concerning the journals may differ from *SRDS*'s and *Bacon's* because of the special interests of the subscribers to these directories. They appeal largely to free-lancers and to their markets. One item that they include is the rate of payment, a matter of no interest to the professional writer who is paid from another source. They may not be suitable for the professional writer who works for an industrial company or a public relations agency. They are surely of no value to the professional writer who has a single paper or article to place in print.

INTERNATIONAL LISTINGS

The primary source for international listings is *Ulrich's International Periodical Directory*, published by R. R. Bowker (a division of Xerox Education Systems). This major, hard-bound directory is issued every few years and includes more listings of journals than all others combined. In order to include all these listings, there is an unavoidable sacrifice in the quantity of data provided. *Ulrich's* is excellent for its listing of professional journals, somewhat less reliable for business and trade publications. It gives titles, frequency, latest known editor, address, circulation, and more. It also gives some indication of the intended readership in many of its listings.

Both *SRDS* and *Ulrich's* include international listings. *SRDS* has relatively few, and most of these are audited publications. (Currently there are few audited journals outside of North America, although the number is increasing.) *Ulrich's* is comprehensive and lists journals that publish in all languages, giving the language of publication.

An interesting feature in *Ulrich's* is its reference to names of publications that have been dropped. If a publication has changed its name, this is sometimes noted. Thus, if you have been familiar with a journal under a name it used in the past, you can generally find out what it is now called. This feature is extremely valuable in relation to the listing of professional journals.

For an author who wants to reach a professional audience, *Ulrich's* is indispensable, being the only reliable reference work of its type in the world. It's important, however, not to use an old directory. Because of the frequency, or rather infrequency, of the directory's publication, an old edition is hopelessly out of date.

Directories of publications are published in other countries as well, but these are seldom as comprehensive or reliable as those published in the United States. The American volumes are to be recommended for authors anywhere in the world in preference to those published elsewhere.

R. R. Bowker, publisher of many books about books, has announced plans to publish a new directory to be called *Magazine Market Place: The Directory of American Periodical Publishing.*

WHAT TYPE OF PUBLICATION IS IT?

Now that you know the name of the journal, you have to find out more about what type of journal it is. Some are self-evident by their names. Others are difficult to categorize. *The Journal of Pathology* is easily identified. A journal for an organization such as the American Chemical Society would not be so easy to classify.

With the latter types of journals, some questions to ask are: What types of articles are covered? Is this a newsletter type of journal, describing where members are and what they are doing? Is it a technical journal that reports on new industrial developments? Is it a highly professional journal that prints only papers delivered at technical meetings and is open to no other contributions but those technical papers given at various ACS seminars and conferences? Unless you know the answers to these questions, you will not know what to do, or will waste a lot of time and effort.

Before you write for some nebulous reader and make contact with an editor of a journal with some unknown (to you) point of view, you should find out what each journal is and does. Each one may be a candidate for your article, or none may be. Before you go too far, eliminate the absolute negatives. Then go after the possibles. From there, you can do further weeding out and concentrate on the probables.

WHOM DOES THE PUBLICATION ACTUALLY REACH?

At this point you may have only titles of journals by which to determine their various audiences. You need more than titles, of course.

One way to get good information is to write to those magazines in which you are potentially interested and ask for a media file. Although you will get more advertising rate information than you want, you will also get a publisher's statement listing the demographic and geographic distribution of the readers. It will generally also list how many of what readers subscribe, on the basis of job title and function.

This is useful information. For example, if your article is about nuclear physics, a publication that reaches purchasing managers in such a highly technical and sophisticated field is probably not of much value to you. By like token, a purchasing magazine that reaches chief engineers may also be useless. You can find out this information from the media file.

Personnel titles can be quite misleading. You may have to know something about the industry you are writing for in terms of its corporate organizational hierarchy. The title of president in a large company involves different duties than the same title in a small, entrepreneurial organization. If you are trying to reach chief engineers, you may do quite well with presidents of small companies as well.

You will have to be something of a detective to ferret out the truth concerning the readership. Talking to the editor is a very useful way to find out; he will seldom misrepresent to a writer. If, however, you represent the interests of an advertiser, you may not receive a full answer. Whatever information you do get will be accurate, though.

SPECIAL ISSUES

Many business magazines publish special-interest issues. These are listed in the editorial calendar for each magazine. One source for finding out such information is *The Mediamatic Calendar of Special Editorial Issues*, published by Media/Distribution Services, Inc. (432 West 55th Street, N.Y., N.Y. 10019). This is published three times a year and lists the special editorial emphasis of hundreds of business publications for a forthcoming third of the year. It is published about two and a half months prior to the first month listed. This would not permit sufficient time for negotiation and writing of articles for the early portion of the period covered; it would for the latter portion. This reference work is sold primarily to advertising agencies for their guidance in placing advertising appropriate to the special editorial content planned for each issue. It is very expensive and is usually available only in the largest public libraries.

Information on special issues is also available directly from the publications themselves. If you get a media kit, such information will probably be included. If it is not, ask the editor if he has any special issues planned on the topic you want to write about.

Getting your article into a special issue is excellent. Specialists in that area will probably keep the issue for future reference. Each time they look at it, they will see your article. Also, because of the special emphasis, your article is more likely to get a complete reading.

READ PART, READ MOST, READ ALL

What do readers actually read in any article?

Most read only the first few paragraphs and then lose interest. This may happen because the topic is not of concern to them, because the opening is dull, because of interruptions while they are reading, or because another item or article on a facing page caught their eye.

Even when readers don't lose interest, they seldom read the

entire article unless the subject is very important or interesting to them. There is not a journal published in which a given article is likely to be finished by more than 50 percent of all readers. If they have to turn a page, they may stop reading, particularly if they must search for the continuation in the rear of the book.

Studies have shown that articles on some topics are read more thoroughly than others. The quality of the writing, unfortunately, has relatively little bearing. The manner in which the article is presented is usually more important than the textual content. So, don't be surprised if you meet people who say they have read one of your articles but who don't remember what it was all about. They may have read some, or read most, but have not read all.

When you look very carefully into the quality of journals you will find that some enjoy better readership than others in terms of the percentage of each article that is actually read. One journal might enjoy a "read most" rating of 70 or 80 percent; another might have only 20-30 percent. These numbers are important to know, if you can get them. It is a very hazy area and it is unlikely that anyone has been able to quantify it. Nevertheless, the data are real, if unobtainable.

The general impression of most readers may be a suitable guide. You might want to turn to some readers of a journal to find this out. When you ask, try to be indirect; few people will readily admit that they do not finish what they start.

READER-SERVICE NUMBERS

For those people who do finish reading an article, there should be some reward. If a reader goes all the way, you can be sure he is truly interested in what you have said. He will probably want to get more information. For this reason, some business magazines include a reader-service number at the end of each article through which additional information might be available.

This is a dual service, helping both the reader and the editor. A journal that has a vibrant editorial approach will attract the active, intense, vital people in an industry. They will tend to read more of an article than people who are just killing time until retirement or who view reading a business or professional magazine as more a matter of recreation than procreation. If there is no way for the active readers to obtain more information, they will often telephone the editor and ask him for names, addresses, and telephone numbers.

This is a nuisance that an editor can ill ignore. For the writer, it can mean a loss of value for his work if there is no way for the reader to get more information. A professional public relations writer who writes an article, or a manager of a company that pays a consultant, wants to obtain maximum value from his investment. A reader-service number enables him to get such a return.

Occasionally, a major article of considerable length will keep readers interested to the end and generate more reader inquiries than very short product and literature releases. If the topic is vital and timely, it will certainly do so. It is not at all unusual for a major article to generate inquiries comprising up to 2 or 3 percent of the total circulation of a journal. I personally have seen several thousand inquiries resulting from a major article of this sort published in a magazine with a circulation of less than 100,000.

PASS-ON CIRCULATION

The average business magazine reaches more than one person. The numbers can range as high as four people per copy, with three per copy a good performance. Professional journals also enjoy some pass-on readership, although not as much as business magazines. Thus, inquiries generally are generated from a readership larger than the base circulation figure.

Some companies and organizations subscribe to a few copies and have routing slips to make certain that a large number of associates and employees get to see the magazines. Some have provision for notations that specific people are to read specific articles. There is no way to anticipate what situation will prevail when you select a journal to approach for your article.

WHAT DO READERS BELIEVE ABOUT THEIR MAGAZINES?

Readers believe in their business and professional magazines. They have made a mental commitment to receive and read the magazines, and they do not like having to question their own judgments. They believe that business and professional magazine editors try to present honest information in a forthright manner. They really do trust these journals, in contrast to the prevalent distrust of general public media. Surveys have firmly established this.

If you present one point of view in an article, the editor may insist that you also present the opposing point of view. You will have armed the reader with ideas that enable him to approach his supervisor with assurance that he can answer both positive and negative questions. In this circumstance, there is good reason for a reader to trust his magazine.

CREDIBILITY AND THE PRESTIGE OF THE PUBLICATION

Not all publications enjoy equal prestige. Not all editors are equal in ability. Not all are equal in their knowledge of an industry or technology. Not all work as hard as others to assure balance in their editorial presentations. Herein lies an important difference among magazines.

When your article appears in a magazine that is held in high esteem by its industry or profession, you enjoy a portion of that prestige. If the editor has chosen to place your article, with your name on it, in his magazine, you will gain only as much prestige as the readers accord the journal. Simply put, you are only as good as the vehicle you ride in.

It behooves you to try to match your objective with the standing of the publication. Don't assume that merely because a magazine is held in high regard, this is the only publication for your article or paper. You may be in the wrong place. High regard and esteem may accrue to a magazine because of the sophistication of its editorial material—and you may not have such material to offer. Prestige may attach to a journal because of the professional standings of members of its editorial staff—and your material may not be suitable. Stay away from such journals if you are not prepared to compete in the same league.

It is also important not to judge a journal's prestige by the subject area covered. Prestige is relative; we are not concerned here with relative social standing. A medical publication is not more prestigious than an automotive publication because doctors are more highly respected than used car dealers. If your story concerns used cars, that is where you belong. Just make sure that the magazine you select is respected for the type of article you have in mind.

When you reach the right magazine, you will automatically reach the right audience, and vice versa.

4

---

find out if the editor
is interested

THE FREE-LANCE WRITER is always advised to approach an editor with an idea and see if the editor is really interested. He is told, in other words, to query the editor.

Staff personnel of public relations agencies and of other types of companies, associations, and organizations are well advised to do likewise. All those who know the workings of the business and professional press advise writers to query editors to learn how they should prepare material for publication, regardless of the writers' own thoughts concerning the apparent appropriateness of their ideas.

Querying pays off. You will seldom get a brush-off. Some editors report that they accept as many as half of the articles for which queries are received. Some report that almost all queries result in articles. On the other hand, some editors report a much lower percentage.

Keep in mind that some publications receive very few inquiries from free-lance and professional writers because of the detailed scientific or technical nature of their audiences. A magazine such as *Quick Frozen Foods* would probably not publish material that would come to the attention of the average free-lance writer.

Professional writers who have something appropriate for that industry will generally be well received.

This type of publication would be very attractive to the professional public relations consultant who finds that a client has developed a peripheral market for which some publicity might be appropriate. In such an instance, the public relations agency should not just send a letter. A phone call is much, much better.

A public relations agent or a company public relations specialist can be viewed as a professional on a par with the editor of the journal, whereas the free-lancer is truly often an amateur, albeit a very good one. Since many professional public relations people have spent time working for the business and professional press, they generally have some knowledge of the proper ways to approach editors. They have only to think of what their circumstances were when they held comparable jobs.

BE HONEST AND COMPLETE

When querying an editor regarding his interest in an article, don't play guessing games with him. If you have a story about a company, name the company and describe the subject and the editorial approach you have in mind, or you might as well not waste your and his time. If you don't provide all the information, he won't know (1) whether the company is or is not in his industry; (2) whether the application, development, or whatever is of interest to his readers; and (3) whether there is likely to be a conflict between what you propose and what someone else may have proposed at almost the same time.

If you want to get an answer that isn't "no," ask a complete question. When you query an editor, you are assuming that he will hold your inquiry in confidence. If you don't feel you can trust him, why bother approaching him at all? Any time you withhold answers to questions that he asks, he will conclude either that you have inadequate information on which to base an article or that you are trying to hide something to get a marginal story published.

ASK ABOUT STYLE

If the editor expresses interest in the subject matter, he will expect that your article will require a minimum of editing by him or his staff. He wants you to do a complete job. Because of demands on his time, he would prefer not to put in the work of editing for style or researching additional material.

By querying the editor before starting your research for writing, you should be able to virtually eliminate all problems of tone, style, and other editorial matters. Ask for a sample of a recent issue of the journal. Ask the editor if he follows or recommends a style guide. Some of the more technical journals use the style guide of the U.S. Government Printing Office. Others will recommend various style guides of the Associated Press, *The New York Times*, and so forth.

Because of the great number of business journals and the hybrid nature of most of them, no single guide will cover all magazines or even all portions of the same magazine. If the publication covers a particular specialty, such as electronics engineering, all symbols and abbreviations will have to conform to the style guide of the appropriate professional engineering association. Follow the guide faithfully.

QUERY ABOUT ORGANIZATION AND ARTWORK

Each editor has devised an expository method with which his readers are familiar. Know it. Ask him if he wants a summary or abstract. Ask if he can suggest a generalized outline to follow. In some cases he may prescribe a specific outline. By following whatever outline he gives you, you will enhance your chances of getting your article accepted.

The editor can also tell you how much commercial material is acceptable. Most reputable journals try to keep company names out of the early paragraphs. Sometimes this will be impossible; the editor will know.

The editor may insist on photographs, may insist that performance data be given in graphic rather than verbal form, or may call for artwork to be prepared in a specific manner.

FACE-TO-FACE QUERYING

You may be fortunate enough to be able to ask an editor face to face if he is interested in your idea for an article. This occasion may arise at a convention or conference, at which time you can "buttonhole" the editor for a few minutes. A few minutes of personal, direct contact can work wonders to assure you a place in a magazine. It is not usually a good idea to ask the editor to join you for a luncheon or some other activity that has to be specially arranged. Most editors will decline to meet with you on the mere prospect of an article, unless there are some other overriding considerations. It is too time-consuming.

USE THE TELEPHONE

If you really want an answer quickly, use the telephone. When the editor is overseas, use telex or cable. There is nothing quite like getting an answer directly from the person who has to make the decision, especially if you get it shortly after you think of the idea. The telephone is direct, personal, and definitive.

Although there are times when letters are appropriate, there are more times when a personal conversation with an editor will be rewarding for both you and him. The main reason for querying the editor is to find out if he is interested in what you have to offer. To make such a decision, he needs a fairly clear idea of what you have in mind. A personal, give-and-take interchange is sometimes much more satisfactory than a series of letters, none of which can reflect a tone of voice, an attitude, an implied agreement, a sense of comprehension and understanding. Remember that all communication is not verbal. As a writer, you know that only too well.

You can negotiate over the phone. Your ideas and those of the editor will not necessarily be the same. You may start out with some misunderstanding of each other's objectives. By the time you put down the phone, you both should have come to a meeting of minds. You will know what the editor wants, how he thinks, what is and is not important to him, what he believes will be acceptable. You will also have established a personal contact that is nearly as valuable as a face-to-face meeting.

If the editor finds your subject matter sufficiently interesting, he may suggest more of an undertaking on your part than you had originally envisioned. He may also know of developments with which you are unfamiliar. He might suggest a meeting with him alone or a meeting at which other people attend. You just can't anticipate what will happen.

If the editor stays on the phone with you for 10 or 15 minutes, he is giving you enough of his time that he clearly feels the investment should pay off for him. If he gives you more than a few minutes, you can assume that he is interested. If he is not, he'll cut you off rather quickly. Once you have spoken with each other, thrashed out problems, and clarified many of the nebulous areas, the editor has made an emotional commitment. This is good for you.

The editor may or may not place your possible contribution on his calendar for future follow-up. He knows that many contributors, or would-be contributors, fail to follow through even after detailed discussions of this sort. Either way, when you do deliver your article, he will recall his conversation with you.

FOLLOW UP WITH A LETTER

A generally profitable but not essential practice is to follow up your phone conversation with a letter. Don't expect the editor to confirm receipt of the letter. He is too busy to answer all such letters and knows from experience that many would-be contributors never deliver their promised articles on time or at all.

In your letter, record the decisions reached during the phone call. That way, if you and the editor have different interpretations of the conversation, he can write back to correct you. The phrase "correct you" implies that the editor is right and you are in error. This may not be truly the case but it is the way things work, so accept it. Whatever the editor believes he said is likely to prevail, even if it is not what he actually said.

By putting the agreements in writing soon after the phone call, you will catch the ideas when they are freshest. Time will not have dulled either your perceptions or those of the editor. He will welcome the letter because it will give him a chance to recall your conversation and may save both of you embarrassment later, when memories have faded.

The editor will probably send you whatever style and other information you want after he gets your letter; your letter constitutes a second—written—request. He might not remember after your phone call, nor will he necessarily ask for your address on the phone. Some editors, incidentally, insist on follow-up letters. A letter gives them a full and correct address and telephone number. It also gets filed with the story reference data, if any. It serves as a hard-copy reminder.

Your letter tells the editor that you are serious about the article you have proposed. If you weren't, you wouldn't have taken the trouble to write a letter. If the phone conversation pointed up some negative aspects of the article, you may want to rethink some of your ideas. A letter gives you the chance to repropose the article with a new approach. If the editor has been less than enthusiastic, your letter may just sway him in your favor. Further, the letter confirms that you will accept his guidance.

In your confirming letter, give dates when you expect to have the article in the editor's hands. Also indicate what types of graphics you propose. This not only confirms the phone conversation, but also gives you a chance to send some sample graphics. If writing samples are needed, they can likewise be enclosed.

Note that with some articles, clearances and approvals have to be obtained. This topic should have been discussed with the editor on the phone, but your letter can be much more specific. You may, after giving the matter some thought, have reached a conclusion that the editor and not yourself is the best person to get the approval.

Take advantage of the letter to make your contact with the editor a more solid one.

"IF I WANTED IT TOMORROW, I'D ASK FOR IT TOMORROW"

A magazine is not a wire service. It does not send telegrams to its readers. Sometimes it is not even particularly timely.

A magazine takes a long time to assemble. Many specialists are involved, each contributing a piece to the whole. A weekly cannot be put together in one week; a monthly takes well over a month; a quarterly may take half a year. Allow for this time factor.

When you plan to submit an article for any particular issue of a journal, be aware of its lead time for preparation. As an example, consider what happens with a monthly journal (Weeklies, bi-weeklies, and journals with other frequencies should be considered in proportion.) For a monthly, if the editor is to plan his magazine, he needs the contributed article no less than two months before the date of issue. That is, if you have promised an article that is to appear in a March issue, you should have it in the editor's hands at least two months before publication.

This sounds simpler than it is because March stretches from the 1st to the 31st. The magazine may come out as much as two weeks before the beginning of the month, that is, around February 14. Or it may come out late in the month, that is, around March 28. This gives you a range of at least 45 days, meaning that you have to get the material to the editor some time between December 15 and February 1. You should find out when, exactly, the editor needs to have the article in final form.

A misunderstanding in this area can lead to serious problems for the editor. Say material is promised for the 28th day of the month (no month stated), and the contributor thinks that this means the month of issue. Imagine going to press late in February, lacking an article that the contributor had believed was due on March 28 because March was the month of issue. This is not at all unusual. As a contributor you can do this to an editor but once.

The best practice is to ask the editor when he wants your article and then meet this deadline with some days to spare. Editors are used to having articles arrive late, so your editor will be relieved when yours arrives early. The staff may be able to get a head start on whatever work is required.

WHAT AND HOW TO TELL THE READERS

You may feel a certain article should be written in a certain way; the editor may feel differently. In fact, if this author's experience is any guide, the editor surely will feel differently. His years on the job have taught him that some editorial approaches work better than others, and some don't work at all. He has also found that he needs variety to keep up reader interest. Sometimes this variety takes the form of writing style, graphics, or both. It is worth finding out which way to "slant" your article.

Slanting, as applied to an article, is not a pejorative term. Slant is a point of view. It is a matter of selecting the important points, placing them in spots that will maximize reader interest, explaining some material in terms the reader is familiar with, or emphasizing some material at the expense of other material in the text.

Your telephone conversation should have given you some idea of the topics the editor wants you to cover. In your letter you will have already given the editor an outline of how you plan to present your subject matter. Then the editor, bless his heart, tells you that he wants you to rework the outline and change the sequence of your material.

What the editor is telling you is that he believes his readers have a particular way they read his magazine. And he often knows exactly what he's talking about. For example, some magazines are more frequently read starting from the rear than from the front because readers know what they will find in the "back of the book," as it is called.

The editor may ask you to write an abstract if readers of the article are used to having this. (Sometimes he reserves this writing for his own staff.) If the editor asks you to put your summary at the beginning, he is implying that his readers do not usually read entire articles. If he tells you that some items should be taken out of the main text and made into separate short articles (called sidebars), he may be trying to shorten the article so the readers will more likely read the entire text. He may tell you to eliminate some material altogether. This may hurt your pride, but the editor's sense tells him that the material won't be received well. Your pride will recover very quickly when the article appears, even if you are not completely pleased with it.

A very important limitation will be the number of words or pictures. There is only so much space in a magazine. Some must be allocated to a variety of articles and subjects; you can get just a limited amount. Don't count on any specific length based on your conception. The article may be worth less or more space according to the editor. Have faith that the editor knows best or he would not be the editor.

As for the writing style, the editor may suggest a first-person approach. This could surprise you, but it might be the best way to put across difficult material. Another approach might be that of an interview, also rare in a contributed article but thoroughly effective.

When the editor plans his magazine, he plans your article as part of it. He may not know for certain when it will appear, and probably will not schedule it until it is complete and in his hands, but he needs a variety of approaches. Knowing what else is likely to be published in the months to come, he may be giving you the opportunity to enjoy the greatest reader interest with a change-of-pace approach.

If what the editor suggests seems too difficult, or you feel that it is inappropriate, then by all means demur. He will understand if you explain your reasons. Don't change the approach without letting the editor know and then submit something different from what he expects and what you have confirmed in your letters.

BYLINES

At times, a writer's company will ask only that the author's byline carry the name of the company. Nowhere else in the article will the company name appear. The prestige that attaches to the authorship suffices to establish the "leadership" of the company. If this can be done, it works very well for author, company, and publication.

This approach is more likely to enhance the image of a company or writer than a more blatant approach. Articles are not for selling; advertising is. Articles are not successful when written for the self-gratification of the author or the author's company. They are valuable only when they serve the interests of the readers as well as or better than they appear to serve the interests of the author.

If a name goes on the article, the onus is very much on the author as concerns the content of the article. You are signing your work, just as an artist signs his canvas. Even though you have your name on the work, the editor may ask for many changes and revisions. He is really an angel, keeping you out of the purgatory of criticism of your colleagues. He is seeking to satisfy the particular interests of his readers. This is especially true of professional publications.

Sometimes this can go too far. There have been occasions when editorial boards were so parochial and uninformed that they could not comprehend new ideas. For example, when the first ideas on quantum physics were disclosed, the initial article on the topic appeared in a fourth-rate Japanese publication because the reviewers on other publications didn't want to have their own pet preconceptions demolished. Even though the author was willing to have his name on an article, he was given almost no opportunity to express his views.

Editors may insist on bylines. In a business journal that seldom carries technical material, a byline would usually be essential on a technical article. This relieves the editorial staff of the journal of the responsibility for substantiating things they know little or nothing about. It also increases reader confidence that the author is someone with considerable knowledge. The expertise of the author is confirmed by his byline.

ALL MAGAZINES ACCEPT NONSTAFF MATERIAL

When you approach an editor, you may be told that his magazine accepts no material from outside its own staff. Don't believe it. Every business and professional publication accepts such material, even the most prestigious magazines, which deny this vehemently. It is the manner in which the material is presented and accepted that constitutes the difference. Some journals publish nothing but bylined materials submitted from contributors; some will accept nothing that has to be credited with a byline.

It is patently impossible to run a publication of any sort without input from a broad range of readers and contributors. Not even a newspaper, with a staff of hundreds, can do this; it cannot possibly have staff everywhere that things happen. Readers call in the news, and then it is followed up. Photographers sell pictures to the paper. Just recall that the only photographs of the assassination of John F. Kennedy were taken by an amateur, not a professional on the spot.

In the case of the business press (and here we may exclude the professional press, since virtually everything published in the professional press is contributed), there is plenty of material "placed" by professional public relations agencies and corporate personnel. It is just not credited to them. Much of it is not in the form of complete articles, but is considered contributed since in form, style, and content it conforms to the requirements of the journal.

Such material seldom is paid for by the magazine; it has already been paid for by the client or the writer's company. Even if it is bylined, it will probably not be paid for.

UNSOLICITED ARTICLES

Every day, hundreds of articles are mailed to editors in the hope that they will be published. These are unsolicited articles: they have not been queried about, are generally not wanted, and are frequently regarded by editors as so much clutter and wastepaper. Few reputable journals will publish them.

Most unsolicited articles have little to do with the business of the journals that receive them. They are often quite broad in scope, relating to business in general and to nothing in particular. With the change of a few words, they can be as appropriate to the hairdressing trade as to the nuclear science industry. Many are blatantly slanted to a particular commercial interest or political viewpoint. A good unsolicited article may find its way into print. A bad one may also, usually in a second-rate journal, to fill space.

Some unsoliciated articles are offset printed and sent to every magazine listed in various magazine directories.

It is impossible for an editor to tell whether an unsolicited article has been offered to him exclusively or whether it is a piece of a blanket mailing. If the technical or business field is very narrow, the editor may take the trouble to find out. He is even more likely to check when the article has come from a reputable company doing business in the industry and the article is about a specific situation in the industry. The editor may even phone the sender if he is astute enough to recognize that he may, in fact, have an exclusive. When he has been sent an original typed copy, he will feel he is on firm ground. If the article has been copied or printed, he may not be.

When the article is good enough for publication, the editor may be able to "promote" an exclusive by accepting the piece only on condition that the author tells all other journals that have been sent the material to abstain. If the leading journal in a field wants to publish and that is the condition it sets, the sender is generally quite pleased that he has reached his mark. Unfortunately, the writer will probably miss more often than he wants by using this scatter-gun approach to all journals.

Sometimes these unsolicited articles come without covering letters, with expensive photographs, and with no name for contact. If the job of tracking down the source is too difficult, the editor will give up easily or not undertake it at all.

An article that has been requested after an inquiry to an editor is a solicited article. It is always welcome. Don't send unsolicited ones.

5

---

exclusives

By THE TIME you have gotten this far in writing articles, you should be familiar with the term "exclusive." There is sometimes confusion about the precise meaning of the word. Is a magazine exclusive something like a product that is carried only in Neiman Marcus department stores and no others? Or does it mean that Neiman Marcus carries the item in Dallas, Lord & Taylor in New York, I. Magnin in San Francisco, and Burdine's in Miami?

If a particular journal covers a very narrow field of technology, an exclusive can mean that it truly is the only publication carrying the story. If, however, the subject matter of the article crosses several industry lines, just as the four stores mentioned above do not sell in each others' geographical areas, then an exclusive can mean something different. No journal ever really has a total exclusive unless it creates the material itself, using its own staff, or contracts for a specific article from a specific author.

For practical purposes, the term "exclusive" means that a journal has rights to first publication. Put another way, the editor has rights of first refusal. If the editor turns down the article, it can be offered to another editor, and so on until some editor agrees to publish the article.

Sometimes a time limit is placed on the first refusal. If the editor does not make a decision within a given period, which is stated to him in advance, the writer is then free to offer the article to another editor on an exclusive basis. If you want to place a time limit on your offer, make this explicit. If you get no response by the stated date, call and find out whether a decision has been reached. When one has not, it is accepted practice that the offer for the article is automatically withdrawn. Request return of the manuscript, if one has been submitted, to prevent unauthorized publication.

TOTAL EXCLUSIVES

A total, or complete, exclusive means that an article is offered to only one journal. Some journals will publish nothing that has been offered to any other journal. They have taken the position that since they reach the cream audience, they need not compromise. Having the courage of their convictions, they tend to create an atmosphere that creates the fact.

Total exclusives are usually negotiated between editor and author. As a rule, if you want to give a total exclusive to a journal you will find yourself promising this value in return for a promise of publication when the article is ready. You probably wouldn't want to write the article ahead of time and then hope that some editor would grant you the privilege of using the pages of his publication. If you do a lot of work prematurely, you might be terribly disappointed if the journal you have your eye on turns you down.

Total exclusives have greatest value when the topic you plan to write about is of interest to either a very narrow audience or a very large group. This will tend to restrict your choice of journals, but it also means the journal that agrees to publish your article will be unique. The advantage of total exclusivity to the journal is that it carries a story not available anywhere else. Your advantage is that you will usually get a more welcome reception from a desirable journal if you offer its editor a total exclusive.

INDUSTRY EXCLUSIVES

Let's assume your proposed article contains references to several industrial or technological fields. You believe that it will interest audiences who read different journals in different industries. You also think very few readers will see the publications from the other industries. Here you may have the makings of an industry exclusive.

Industry exclusives are usually negotiated following the writing of the article. In this case you needn't be as concerned about which journal in the industry publishes your material. Always start with the most highly regarded magazine and offer an industry exclusive to that journal, with the understanding that you are also offering the article to journals in other fields. You must promise not to offer the article to competing magazines in the editor's industry, subject to first refusal. Give one editor a chance to refuse before you approach another. If you violate the concept of exclusivity, you may never have another chance to publish in a reputable journal that you have slighted.

Say you have written an article about the use of a computer in the baking industry to handle specialized personnel problems that are unique to that industry. You can offer your article on an industry-exclusive basis to a computer publication, a baking industry magazine, and a journal concerned with personnel relations. The overlap of readership would be almost nil. The editors would not quibble about the exclusive.

ARE EXCLUSIVES WORTHWHILE?

This is a hard question to answer. The answer is really both "yes" and "no," depending on where you sit.

Exclusives are worthwhile because some editors will not deal in any other way. It may be the only way to get your article published. If you approach an editor of the journal that is most highly regarded in its field and he asks for an exclusive or "no go," you must give it to him.

In return for the exclusive, the editor will give you some

editing and negotiation time. The article that you plan to write no longer becomes an "off the shelf" item. It is a solicited and custom-crafted product. The editor may also become a friend. Once you have honored your commitment, he will consider your word excellent and will probably accept more articles from you.

Exclusives are certainly worthwhile for editors, since the latter will have something for their readers that can be found in no other journal. Exclusives are always worthwhile for the magazine. They are worthwhile for the writer only if he intends to write other articles for the journal at some future date. Sometimes the "writer" is a company with many scientists, engineers, or other specialists who write articles. In this case, the exclusive may be the only way for the company to deal. Professional public relations personnel prefer exclusives for a variety of reasons, as will be discussed in Chapter 16.

A VALUELESS EXCLUSIVE

An exclusive is valuable to you only if it may help you to place your article in the best journal. If you offer your best efforts to a second-rate journal on an exclusive basis, you may gain little prestige by the exposure.

Some editors will publish material that has appeared in other, competing journals because it is easy to get. Or they will find some obscure journal overseas and pirate the material in violation of copyright laws that both countries subscribe to. If you offer your material to such journals on an exclusive basis, you will gain nothing and lose much.

Another valueless exclusive—really not an exclusive at all—is the one you offer to an editor and then tell him that you have divided his industry so narrowly that half the journals he considers competitive have been given the material, also on an "exclusive" basis. Expect a refusal here.

Be prepared to tell an editor which journals you have submitted, or offered to submit, your material to. If he wants to consider your article for publication, he may insist that you withdraw the offer from the other magazines in exchange for guaranteed publication in his magazine.

AN EXCLUSIVE SHOULD BE UNIQUE

Sometimes an exclusive technically exists and yet does not meet one of the most important criteria for an exclusive: the appearance of being exclusive. This will occur when two virtually identical stories appear in two different, competing publications simultaneously. Only the names or locations are different; the subject is the same.

True, each is an exclusive. Yet neither one is truly unique. Uniqueness is the hallmark of the exclusive, the reason why it is so desirable. To provide competing publications with stories that are similar in all aspects except for, perhaps, the names of the equipment users is to violate the spirit of exclusivity.

A company or writer who attempts to capitalize on a designation of "exclusive" will find that this type of approach is not very welcome. Readers cannot distinguish the fine points, and should not be expected to. You, however, as the author, should know the distinctions and respect them. It is not enough for your exclusive to just meet the letter of the requirement; test to see if it meets the spirit as well. If it does not, don't represent your efforts as exclusive.

IS THE COVER AVAILABLE?

In exchange for an exclusive of real value, an editor may be willing to use some of your material if it is suitable for a front cover. If you have such material, try to grab this offer. Such an opportunity comes rarely and gives you tremendous future merchandising value. All you have to pay for is the material that goes onto the cover. The journal pays for the cost of separations (if color) and the cost of printing and artwork that relate to the cover itself but not to your specific material. Remember, a magazine can publish 10 or more articles in a single issue but it has only one front cover.

Ask the editor if he needs material for a cover. Think of it this way: you have offered to give him an exclusive article. You wouldn't have risked this unless you knew his publication and knew the type of article he would want. You should also know his cover requirements, even if only slightly. Be brazen. You can only get turned down, and it will be a polite turndown. If you don't ask, you probably will get no cover.

FILLERS

If you have a very short article, the type that can fit on a page or less when printed, don't bother with an offer of exclusivity. Editors always need this type of material to fill pages. They cannot normally schedule it in advance, but it is something they will hold in type just in case of emergency. These items really are "fillers," also called "shorties" or "shorts." They come in very handy when an advertiser fails to get his material in on time and space has to be filled. They also work well when an article that was expected to run three pages ends up running only two and a half.

The best type of subject matter for the short article is an application story. A brief case history is easy to read. It tells all in less than 500 or 600 words, and it has a picture or two. Two typewritten pages and two illustrations will cover the subject. You can get a very good reception with this type of article.

You do not need to query an editor about a short article. Just send it as you would a press release (see Chapter 14) and provide all necessary information for contact.

DO EXCLUSIVES PAY?

A publication will generally pay you for material that is totally exclusive and which is written to order. You will never receive payment for an article that is submitted to a dozen journals. Payment policies vary from journal to journal, but nobody ever gets paid by a magazine unless the material was totally committed to that one outlet.

Professional public relations personnel need not be concerned with payment policies. They are paid by their clients, and they seek the widest audiences possible, consistent with the value of such readers to their clients' interests. Usually they would not receive payment from a magazine unless the publication had a rigid policy of paying all contributors. Such policies are rare.

Scientists, engineers, specialists, marketing people, and others who work for industrial and commercial companies may receive payment from a publication, depending on the publication's policies. If the article is one that cannot be written by the staff of the journal because of its complexity and technical detail, a contributor is more likely to be paid than if the article is one that describes the favorable experience of a user of a company's products.

Some companies pay their own personnel to write, and rely upon their staff public relations personnel to try to place the articles. Under such conditions, a journal is not likely to pay the author. It is assumed that the material has been reviewed, revised, and approved to meet the commercial ends of the company. Although such material is valuable for readers, it is too commercial to be completely impartial. The editor may insist on a total exclusive for such material, but he will not pay for it.

6

types of articles

PRIOR TO A DISCUSSION of the various types of articles, it may be helpful to discuss people's motivations for having articles published. Why should anyone want to write? For some authors, this is simply a line of work that they find comfortable and compatible with their personalities. If they are free-lance writers, this may be their only source of income; they need to write to put food on the table. And then there is the desire, the very human desire, for recognition. Recognition and approbation are often what are sought when a writer is eager to see his name in print. Sometimes he is less interested in seeing his name in print than in having other people see it in print. This is often the motivation of people who write letters to the editors of their local newspapers.

Some people write just to keep their names known to their colleagues. Often they are technicians who have done independent work or have achieved recognition for proficiency in a specialty. Since these specialists usually have material of genuine value to offer their colleagues, editors seldom impute ulterior motives. Such motives, in fact, may be absent in many instances. Editors are happy to be able to get such competent editorial material. As established writers, these specialists also tend to have a good understanding of the needs of editors. Their material is usually quite good.

Another motivation to write and be published may stem from the legal necessity to prove that a development has taken place at a given time and in a given place. The published article can later be cited when legal action is undertaken. A firm or individual may wish to document commercial actions that have been taken, prior art or a discovery, or disclose a major scientific event. Legal disclosure is here the motive for writing and publishing. Publication in an independent journal provides a large measure of legal protection.

People who run businesses often want to earn the respect of their customers and potential customers. They like to have articles appear about their company, its work, its products, its services, its personnel, its financial strengths (never its weaknesses)—in general, its most favorable attributes. This improves the firm's image and makes business easier to conduct—translating into more income with less expense. It certainly is an understandable and realistic motive. Sometimes, the nature of the business can justifiably be criticized, but this question should be raised only when a specific editorial situation has to be evaluated.

Members of a scientific research group, educational institution, or similar organization will want to have their findings published because this justifies the faith, and dollars, of those who contribute to their upkeep. Publication is the only way they can inform their benefactors of the quality and scope of their work. A published internal document is seen by too few of these philanthropists; it is useful only for other specialists who take the trouble to seek it out. Publicity is the motive here.

This brief recital of motives is certainly not exhaustive. The aspiring author needs to harness the energies that drive him to write and use these energies to make sure he writes in a manner that is acceptable to the editor and the reader. Otherwise, all this effort will have been wasted. An author's writing technique can vary according to his motivation.

Regardless of the writing technique employed, the final article is one that can be classified into one of several types. Descriptions of some classifications follow.

CLASSIFYING ARTICLES BY TYPE

Any system for classifying articles will be somewhat artificial, since there is always overlap. For our purposes, it is most useful to refer to articles in the way most editors generally refer to them. These types of articles are given descriptive names for convenience only. Some may be known by other names as well. Most editors will understand what you mean if you use these terms. Here is a brief listing of types of articles, not necessarily in order of complexity or desirability for publication:

Documentation
Introduction to new technology
Introduction to a new application
How to do something
How the other fellow does it: the case history
State-of-the-art report
Roundup
Problems and solutions
Ideas and concepts
General business

The foregoing list is not intended to represent an achievement ladder in a technology or science, but developments do tend to follow in the order listed. Generally a subject is first reported as an achievement or development in a research area. Then comes material explaining how the achievement could be applied in a practical sense, followed by step-by-step explanations of ways of using it to gain its benefits. Should some astute professionals or technologists apply the new concept successfully, a report on how they have prospered would be in order. This report would provide encouragement to others to follow. Once the technology has progressed and proliferated, so many individuals would be involved that it would become impossible to keep up with the great variety of approaches taken by all these people. This is the time for some sort of assurance to the reader that he is not unique in his ignorance or his limited knowledge. It would be appropriate to place all the developments in perspective by means of comparisons with related developments.

From what we said earlier, it would appear that the reader of business or professional journals is a specialist. This is usually true. Because he is a specialist he cannot be expected to know everything about the newest developments that may come along, except those in his narrow area of specialization. He would certainly lack familiarity with new peripheral developments. He may be working in such a specialized area that he does not even normally come into contact with certain mainstream developments.

Short public relations materials, such as product or literature releases, are not included in this classification system because they are not articles. They are announcements and will be treated separately in Chapter 14.

Documentation

Most work in science and industry results from some prior research. New work that is to be announced in the professional or business press requires a sound and solid basis, a grounding in precursive work that is accepted by colleagues of the writer. (Here we are speaking of the author of the article as being the author of the work described in it. This, of course, is not always the case. The descriptions may be written by technical writers, ghostwriters, public relations staff personnel, consultants, free-lancers, and others.)

Work that advances the state of the art needs to be documented in published form, in terms that are readily comprehensible to the reader. The documentary article is written either to establish the credentials of the author or to place the author's work in its proper place in the hierarchy of current developments.

A documentary article must always start with a description of the point of departure of the work and must not draw conclusions. It assumes that both the writer and the reader are equally knowledgeable and therefore provides only evidence or data that will enable the reader to judge the validity and importance of the work. In this regard, the documentary article differs from all others. Other types of articles may or may not state conclusions (which may actually be only surmises by the author); the documentary article cannot presume to present the author's thinking as to the consequences or value of his work. To do so would not only be in poor taste but might involve poor judgment.

Most authors of documentary articles are asked by editors to provide abstracts of their findings. With some professional publications, this is an absolute requirement. The abstract introduces the material to the reader and provides librarians and other researchers with a synopsis for easy reference. The abstract may be written either before or after the article is completed. Usually it is best composed afterward, when all the data and approaches have been confirmed and the relative importance of various information has been committed to writing.

The documentary article is usually, but not always, organized as follows: abstract, introduction describing point of departure, conditions of research, work performed (presented in either chronological or developmental sequence), findings, and proposed follow-on lines of endeavor. A summary is optional.

Introduction to New Technology

New technological developments seldom take place in a research atmosphere. They are the result of deliberate commercial efforts to create new business opportunities. Where a documentary article will follow lines of exposition very similar to those of a speech (many are actually revised from speeches), the article describing the introduction of new technology is similar in form to a sales presentation.

A sales presentation tells the customer what the purported benefits of a product or service are and what benefits he might expect to accrue to him. If the salesman does not promise the customer at the outset what he will do for him, the customer will probably lose interest. An article must follow the same line of development. The promise must precede the reasoning behind that promise.

This type of article finds greatest acceptance in the business press, although you might consider submitting such a piece to the professional press if a particular publication publishes articles which take the practical (application) approach. If you choose to write this type of article, avoid the more esoteric scientific journals.

As a guide, if a journal does not carry advertising, do not propose this type of article. If the journal carries advertising, the readers will probably be interested in day-to-day information about industrial and commercial applications. This type of article may suggest circumstances under which the technology might be applied, although the knowledge necessary to make practical use of it may not yet have been generated.

The opening of such an article must contain an implied promise of valuable information to follow, valuable in the sense that the reader could put the information to some potential use. The opening, therefore, should summarize advantages and benefits that the reader can suppose will be his to enjoy if he employs the technology which is described.

The writer may, following the opening, choose to take any number of different approaches. These will be determined by the subject matter. One good approach is to follow the summary of benefits with a description of the manner in which the technology could be employed. This would then be followed by more detailed information, including documentation-type data. This ordering of material gives the reader confidence that the claims made have been arrived at by a rigorous scientific method and can be substantiated and duplicated.

If the author desires, the end of the article could be a restatement of the conclusions. Most likely, few readers will get that far. Only the most interested will proceed into the detailed documentation, and they don't always need a restatement of the summary. Business readers go only as far as they need to in order to support their work and supplement their knowledge.

Introduction to a New Application

Some articles describe a new application of an existing product, system, or concept. The article may either describe the new application or imply an endorsement of the application by the originator or an early new user. The aim is to show that a respected user has made a purchase and is pleased with it. An implied endorsement is by far the best type of approach a commercial company can use when having articles written by consulting public relations personnel.

Sometimes a user will not wish to endorse a product, either directly or by inference. Reasons for reluctance vary, but generally the person or company fears competitors will follow suit and will gain similar benefits without having invested similar time, effort, and money. Other reasons for reluctance include a desire to maintain a working distance from a supplier for "leverage," should anything go wrong in the near future; a general desire to maintain a low public profile; a reluctance to reward any specific individual in the company with an accolade that must shortly be followed with additional financial remuneration; a reluctance to publicize the special expertise of a company employee, who may then be sought out by competitors; or a desire to avoid implied criticism of company personnel who have been unsuccessful with the product through no fault of their own.

If an endorsement can be obtained, it should be noted as soon as possible in the article, preferably in the first paragraph. In any case, the first paragraph should indicate the benefits that have accrued to the user. If these benefits are of interest to a reader, he will continue to read; if not, he will stop there.

An article about an application of a product or service is much like a news story. From the opening to the end, the material should be presented in descending order of importance, in terms of value and utility to the reader. One measure of importance is the degree of applicability of the data supplied. The more specific the application data, the less important they become to an individual reader. The more benefit-oriented the information, the more important it is. Leave the technical, detailed data until the end; only the most ardent reader will go that far. Once you have such a reader entranced by the story, you will have reached a potential customer and may have opened the door to a sales contract.

The How-To Article

How-to articles are useful vehicles for companies that wish to demonstrate expertise but cannot make a forthright commercial pitch. By means of such articles, the companies imply an un-tapped depth of technical expertise and a reservoir of talented personnel. Of course, the examples given are favorable to the writer's company.

Because how-to articles are expected to cover a broad technical spectrum, some writers have found that mention of competing or related products increases credibility. Editors may insist on such a balance in order to assure that the data cited will not be viewed as the exclusive province of a particular company or organization. Editors sometimes use data supplied by a number of companies to assemble how-to articles. Here the finished article represents a compilation of data. In this manner, the editor forestalls any accusation that he favors a particular advertiser, supplier, company, organization, or philosophy.

It is just as erroneous to assume that all knowledge and intelligence reside in a single company as to assume that it resides in a single individual. The wise writer will make use of data from a large group of representative supplier companies. This technique is very effective public relations, provided the writer shows off his or her company's achievements as being superior to the others, not in so many words but by other means. One way of doing this is to use photographs supplied by the sponsoring company for major technical points and to use photos of competing companies for the minor points. If the company's achievements are inferior to those of the competitors, the article is best left unwritten. There is no merchandising or prestige value in being second-rate.

How-to articles border on the instructional but should not be didactic. A didactic tone will quickly alienate the reader and lead him to turn his attention elsewhere. The reader likes to feel that he is being informed rather than being instructed, particularly when he believes he has a sound grasp of the material.

Ways of presenting this type of information vary only with the ingenuity of the writer. Consider using some of the following presentation techniques: question-and-answer method, description of a training program, description of existing but rarely used applications, discussion of developments in a manner that provides analysis and synthesis, and more.

How the Other Fellow Does It

How does the other fellow do it? This is a favorite type of article of industrial companies. It is the ultimate testimonial. It tells what the other company, the reader's competitor, does and implies that the reader and his company would enjoy similar benefits. Readers generally like these types of articles.

The opening of an article of this sort should be carefully paced. A rapid, newsy opening with emphasis on the benefits would seem too high pressure and commercial. It is better merely to suggest that the using company has solved a problem. In some instances, half the story might be told before the discussion of the problem is even commenced. This would move the reader into the heart of the article. The description of the solution might appear very late in the telling.

Readers tend to empathize with competitors who have problems. They will be aware that the article will eventually offer a suggested solution. Given a good statement of the problem, an approach to a solution, and then the solution, the reader will follow the entire text. Stated another way; tell them what you are going to tell them, tell them, and tell them what you told them.

To lose a reader at the beginning because he cannot empathize with the problem is to lose little or nothing. The reader who has no awareness of such a problem will never be a prospect for a solution. Conversely, if the reader has a problem, he will go to great lengths to solve the problem and prove himself a hero to his company and to himself.

This type of article should not be rushed. Preparation itself may take quite some time. An editor may want the story to focus on the experiences of one user rather than another, although an article about either may have the same future merchandising value to the writer. The editor may even suggest which user's experience to deal with in order to help the writer get the best reader reaction or public relations value.

In the writing itself, a logical unfolding works best. A lapse of logic during the course of the presentation will probably distress the reader and cause him to lose interest. There must be an unfolding, as in the telling of a mystery story, with the solution given only at the end. Like a sales presentation, the article must continue to hold the interest of the customer if the message is to reach its mark and the sale is to be closed.

State-of-the-Art or Roundup Articles

There are differences between state-of-the-art articles and roundup-type articles. These differences are in content and sometimes in approach. For our purposes they are more alike than different, and so are placed in a single category.

Writing a roundup or state-of-the-art article on a particular technology is normally the responsibility of the staff of the business publication. Nevertheless, this can be written by a supplier to the industry, if the supplier is impartial and can obtain the cooperation (either with the assistance of the editor or directly) of all major competitors.

When a company is well ahead of the field in a specific science or technology, it can afford to promote such an article. If not, this is the worst possible approach to take. Because this type of article implies greater knowledge on the part of the writer than on the part of anyone else who might be qualified to write it, the writer must be able to provide unique data that have never before been presented in print in such an organized and logical fashion. Although the data will not necessarily be new to the reader, the presentation should enable him to gain a new perspective.

If the writer cannot offer this type of assurance, he should stay away from this type of writing. This sort of article is the most complex and time-consuming of all to write. It must be complete. Lack of important data will destroy the credibility of all other data given. An article of this sort may take more than a year to write. It is read intently by a wide spectrum of a publication's readers. It also generally becomes a standard reference.

Claims of completeness must be proved within the article itself. Few readers would believe that any one person has access to all possible data on a topic, so when completeness is sought, it is better to have the publication's editors place their names on the article and take responsibility for its contents.

When the time comes to merchandise the article for commercial advantage, the companies that have provided data can use the comparative information for whatever ends they wish. Many companies will not find this type of article suitable for merchandising. Others will find, to their surprise, that they come off very well in this comparative situation.

There is no particularly logical beginning, no special logical end to this type of article. It starts where the art starts and ends where the art ends. It covers developments that are here and now, not in the future. It covers little of the past except as an introduction to the present.

When a company is asked to contribute data, it will find that such data will be shown separately from data supplied by other companies. Although the data may be placed in comparative form in charts and tables, they still remain isolated, unique, and ascribable to the particular source. It is good business to contribute to such articles when requested to by an editor. Omission of your company's name may imply a lack of commitment to the industry or may lead an editor to infer that you are reluctant to provide data because the data are unfavorable.

Problems and Solutions

Here is a perfect vehicle for a company wishing to promote its expertise. Any company or organization that has any knowledge to impart can use the problem-solution type of article. Most business journals will publish this type of information, particularly if they serve technical fields where application information is required. If many suppliers to an industry or technology have to maintain technical service staffs, the industry will have business publications that welcome this type of article.

Readers look to problem-solution articles for ideas on how to do their jobs better. Often, managerial personnel make sure their operating-level personnel are familiar with the information contained in such articles. One answer in just one article to a question that has troubled company management will more than justify the annual subscription price of a journal.

Ideas and Concepts

Here an engineer, scientist, lawyer, or accountant presents a beautifully worked out thesis—an argument complete with documentation, references, and mathematics—for the purpose of proving a particular concept or idea. This is the technical paper or the oral presentation issued in printed form. It makes excellent and fascinating reading. Everybody wants to get into the argument, if only vicariously. Nobody can get hurt; everyone can have an opinion; each author can cite chapter and verse.

In a sense, this type of article represents an attempt at documentation. But it fails to fit into that classification because the author and readers really are not trying to prove a new fact; they are debating old ideas. Such articles are sometimes referred to as "argumentative," since despite their documentary tone, the purpose is to establish primacy of ideas. These articles also tend to be explicatory, describing actions that have been taken, generally as justification for a particular point of view or philosophical position. Since most scientific research involves some philosophical concepts, any article of this sort will present a point of view to which readers can take exception—and they probably will, in the form of letters to the editor and requests to publish articles presenting opposing points of view.

As will be seen in Chapter 8, this type of article is organized and presented somewhat differently from the foregoing types. Sometimes it originates as an oral presentation and is then modified by the author for the print medium. Even when this is not the case, it may read like an oral presentation. Editors sometimes choose not even to edit such material, except to bring it into conformity with the journal's style. They may just provide an introduction in which the journal states that it neither advocates nor justifies any conclusions reached.

In this type of article, the author marshals his facts. He builds up his case item by item, setting up his "straw men" and demolishing them along the way. Having refuted the logic of opposing points of view, he stands triumphant on the pinnacle of a single idea, claiming to have proved beyond a shadow of doubt that his point of view should prevail.

If the argument has not proved the idea beyond the shadow of a doubt, readers will be quick to point this out and will excitedly encourage each side to do more battle. These debates make for great readership. Every editor would like to be able to offer his journal as a prize ring, with the readers cheering and booing at ringside. All the editor has to do is to referee; he never gets into the fight.

This type of article is suitable for medicine, law, engineering, business, philosophy, the social sciences, and many other fields. It is very difficult to write well and should be left to technical experts because of the vast knowledge it calls for. Since it is essentially argumentative, it deals with ideas that are still under contention in a field. No editor will knowingly take sides against any group of his readers; no editor will ever have this type of article written by his staff.

General Business

Under this heading could be grouped articles about customer service as a unique function, unusual and complete laboratory facilities, plant and facilities expansions (but only when these involve the introduction of new concepts; when the story does nothing more than puff up the importance of a company, readers turn the pages quickly), new enterprises that extend the scope of a business or industry, and specialized financial topics, such as a discussion of how new tax laws will affect a specific industry. With this type of article, it is especially important to discuss the proposed approach with the editor in advance to make sure the article will be directed to the proper market.

Most reputable journals tend not to accept general business articles if they are submitted by companies or their public relations agencies. These are far too suspect in tone and motive. Readers may even begin to suspect that the writer's company is trying to bargain for free publicity in exchange for past or future advertising.

SOME TYPES OF ARTICLES ARE POISON

Do you want to collect rejection letters? Then try this one.

One type of article that readers view with particular cynicism is the recitation which purports to describe a complete operating installation. This sort of piece offers no apparent or implied benefit to the reader. It generally is replete with names and addresses of manufacturers of equipment and suppliers of services, giving no indication of the value of the items described.

This type of article is popular with many advertisers because it is free publicity for them. They like to see their names and products featured prominently in photographs and discussed in detail in the text. It is almost always staff-written, or is contracted for if staff editors cannot go to the location of the installation. Since it is written to flatter advertisers, it can be assumed that staffers know best which advertisers to flatter.

Not surprisingly, readers find this type of article dull, essentially uninformative, and totally suspect. It is one of the very few types of articles in which there is a wide divergence between the interests of the readers and the interests of the journal. The fact is that, except for these types of articles, there are few other such conflicts of interest—that speaks well for the business press's ability to fulfill its basic mission.

Other types of articles can also be written that are counter-productive. Often these constitute a deliberate attempt to place material in the journal with an ulterior motive, rather than to help the readers. Generally, any form of presentation that does not serve the interests of the readers will not serve the interests of either the author or the magazine.

AVOID SOME PROMOTIONAL APPROACHES

There is no set rule concerning which types of articles will be acceptable and which types will be unacceptable for a particular journal. Some editors will publish stories of new manufacturing facilities installed by major industry suppliers. These articles purport to demonstrate how the new facilities or capabilities will enable greater customer service, ostensibly to convince the reader of the value of such an installation to him. They can also be couched as advances in the state of the art. Generally, they are written in a manner more appropriate to the style of a report to stockholders, which relates how wonderful company management is.

These types of articles find their way to business magazines from company public relations departments or public relation agencies. They are never solicited. They sometimes arrive at the editor's desk as a result of prior negotiations, but they never arrive in a form anticipated by the editor. Nevertheless, some of these types of articles may be acceptable to some editors. Definitely query the editor first.

Even if the editor is willing to accept a promotional piece, it is advisable to be cautious because most readers will not be so forgiving. A company that wishes to create a good public image will not achieve this in journals that publish much of this type of material. Such publications are not held in high esteem.

Some journals will devote editorial pages to stories about industry leaders. This is fine when the people written about are actually among the leaders. When they are all advertisers in the journal, readers will suspect the motives behind the article.

It is often the manner in which a subject is handled rather than the subject matter per se that indicates whether the editor has prostituted himself for the promise of financial gain through advertising. Self-praise has a proper place in a business magazine—in the advertising pages.

7

---

choosing your
data sources

SOMETIMES the "author" of an article is a team comprising many people, each one of whom is a specialist and only one or two of whom will actually have their names appended to the article when it is published. This is often the case with a report on research or an article dealing with complex interactions in technology. Such an article requires the combined knowledge and talents of a number of people who have worked together to establish the data or who must work together to write the article.

Members of the team may be related to each other in a pyramid of responsibilities. One person may work for a company, another may be a supplier to that company, and yet a third could be a professional public relations consultant who has been asked to put the article together. This last person may be a specialist also, relatively at home with and knowledgeable concerning the subject matter of the article.

Or he may simply be a ghostwriter (in reality, a member of the team), who does the writing for the technologists, drawing on their knowledge and verifying interpretations with them, much as an editor does when he writes an article.

Sometimes these ghostwriters, or "hired pens," are the people who make the contacts with the editors, evaluate and select possible media for publication, pursue all the necessary steps to completion, and submit the final article. During this process they submit their material to the nominal "author," who actually serves only as a technical adviser and editor, making necessary corrections and changes.

At other times, the "ghost" is the only author and the nominal author has no part in the preparation of the article except to approve it. Frequently, the byline is given as a form of honorarium to a high-level corporate or organization official.

When a number of people are involved in a writing project, complexity enters. It is essential to clarify the roles of each. One person may generate data while another researches supporting material. One may select details from the documents while another develops an outline and places the material in a hierarchical order for reference. One may know where documents can be found; another gets them. And so forth. In any team effort of this nature some members will be deeply involved in researching data while others will evaluate the worth of those data.

SEEKING THE SOURCES

Whether the writing is done by the person whose name appears on the article or by a surrogate, the task of obtaining all appropriate source data is sometimes monumental. This, of course, is far more difficult for a ghostwriter or corporate public relations person than for the researchers who are reporting their own findings. It is always difficult for an outside public relations agency or consultant to know where all suitable data sources may lie. Obviously, distance in time or miles from the original work increases the difficulty of obtaining and validating data.

Surprisingly, data are sometimes made available to public relations consultants more readily than to company personnel. In-house personnel are expected to know where to look, and anyway they are being paid whether their search takes a bit longer or a bit shorter. Outsiders are expected to have more difficulty collecting data than in-house personnel, and they are frequently paid by the time they require, so they are often accorded assistance of a sort not given to insiders. The firm that possesses the needed data may be more helpful to the outsider because it has called in the outsider to work on a project that it wishes to use to enable it to create a good public relations image. It is sometimes believed that this can be done better by outside specialists than by corporate personnel.

One obvious consequence of not having good source data is a poor article. However well written it is, such an article will fail to make the proper impact on readers. Without good data it will fail to impress the editor, even if he himself is not a technical expert in the field. Certainly, the readers will be more technically qualified than the editor, but the editor can spot weaknesses. He will have enough technological knowledge to be able to roughly evaluate the material submitted to him and be aware of how well the sources are known in the industry or the technological field. An astute editor who lacks deep technical knowledge may sense weakness by the manner in which ideas or words are strung together or by the author's failure to make appropriate references.

Sources of data are innumerable. They exist in many places within companies, within research groups, and in the files maintained by individual scientists, technicians, professionals, and sales personnel. Surprisingly, an author who is also a technical expert may at times not know where to seek data that he himself has created. He overlooks the obvious. He is so familiar with the concept and its implementation that he finds himself recreating that which he had put into words earlier. He might recall his prior work but not consider some of it to be sufficient documentation because it was presented in a different form or was not classified in a recognizable or accustomed manner.

SPEAK TO THE TECHNICAL WRITER

It may be helpful to seek out the technical writer or writers, if any, who have been involved at various times in the project. These are people who have solid technical knowledge and are also competent writers. They can take material from engineering data, and provide verbal descriptions of electrons running from place to place. They may read or write proposals and handle the technical or management data the proposals contain. They may assist advertising departments with interpretations, but generally only when asked and only when the informal communications network in the company or organization makes this possible. They can write instructional materials, brochures, data sheets, formal technical presentations, or management presentations. They can work with graphics and are skilled in generating and reading schematics, charts, graphs, photographs, exploded views, parts catalogs.

Technical writers generally know about production and printing methods and know the best ways of presenting material for publication. In fact, they are publication specialists. They will know how adaptable some of their skills are to the article you propose to publish. To the detriment of their companies, technical writers are all too frequently shunted into engineering departments, where much of the public relations contributions they could make to their companies is lost.

Before starting your own search for data sources, go to the technical writing department. The tech writer may already know of sources that would never occur to you. He may have worked on an entire series of documents pertaining to a project, from proposal on through progress reports, instruction manuals, technical brochures, data sheets, and catalogs. In fact, he may actually know more about the project than the project engineer. Since he probably had to assemble much information for review by the project engineer, he may have enjoyed greater rapport with members of his organization over an extended period of time. He will certainly know which individuals have the best information and who can provide it to you in the most logical form.

Sometimes, because of the specialized nature of the work they are involved in, technical writers do not know of all data sources that are available. Basically they are an underrated fount for information and should be referred to at the start. They can save you much unnecessary work with just a few minutes of conversation.

"JUST THE FACTS"

Just trying to establish all the appropriate sources of unimpeachable data for an article can be extremely difficult and frustrating. With the help of specialists, such as technical writers who are not themselves directly involved with the work being reported on, you may get a head start.

Be sure to consider all the sources at your disposal. Unfortunate is the author who lacks knowledge of where to look. Sources are usually so numerous that the problem should be not where to find the information but how to limit the search to a few definitive sources. At the outset, make a list of all documents or sources you believe might be valuable to you. Note the location of these sources, such as advertising department, engineering department, legal department, patent attorneys, field service organization, or elsewhere. At this point, you still have not even seen such documents to evaluate their worth to you.

Bear in mind that data do not have to be written to be useful. Important information is sometimes found in visual aids, physical hardware, taped interviews, and even oral presentations and demonstrations.

If you have already collected the documents for similar, prior research, you will certainly have to reverify the facts for each new article you write. Sometimes, two documents emanating from the same source have contradictory information. The only way to evaluate which one is correct is to go back to an original source. If you have dated material, this may help, but it should not be considered an infallible indicator of correctness. A later publication date doesn't always mean more reliability or greater accuracy of data.

The degree of corporate interest in a document may also serve as an indicator of accuracy. Management will require more effort to be expended in verifying data when these data are of special concern to it. When these data are presented in documents that reach a public that management must deal with, you can be sure that more thought and review will be lavished on such documents. Certainly, any document that is designed to be read by the financial community will be carefully scrutinized. This contrasts, for example, with a lesser interest in a speech to be given by a member of the technical staff to students at a nearby engineering college.

You will find that your list is much like the periodic table of chemical elements: similar and related items have to show up in certain places. As you prepare such a list you will get a sense of whether additional documentation is needed. You will be able to find it more easily with this type of list.

TURNING ROCKS OVER

Now you know what sources to investigate and what specific documents to start with. You have to estimate your ability to get at those documents and sources. Some would take so much time and effort to reach or uncover that they are virtually worthless. Some are so obvious that they may be overlooked precisely for that reason. The most difficult situation of all is when the apparent facts are themselves really only interpretations or opinions. It may be necessary to obtain a sampling of definitive interpretations or opinions. Sometimes you will plan to provide your own interpretations of various opinions but must back up your ideas with solid data that others can review, even if they choose to draw different conclusions. Don't ever accept one person's interpretation concerning the work of another if you can go directly to the source.

There is one bright spot in all of this: most companies in the same line of business tend to generate similar material in similar forms. For example, annual reports of companies in the same business usually contain the same types of information, even if it is not assembled in an identical fashion. This advantage is too often overlooked.

In other instances, data must be sought from a different industrial, commercial, or scientific field. Here it is hard to get correct information, unless you know exactly what data sources to go to.

Many articles are written well before formal data on the topic have been generated, organized, and published. Therefore, some data sources may not yet exist. However, if an author has reached the point of planning to write a definitive article, a large corpus of different types of documentation will exist, whether he or others originally generated the data. When limited data are available on your topic or you are limited in your access to the data, you may be in a position where you are going to create some basic documentation with your article. The paper will then become an important source of data for other researchers, writers, or technicians. Sometimes publication is sought precisely because the author has recognized a need to document. This situation can provide a fascinating challenge for any writer.

DATA SOURCES OVERLAP

Sometimes related data may be carried in several locations, apparently overlapping. For instance, a full-line product catalog may contain a bound-in price list or detailed technical explanations of new products. Application data appear in numerous places: application notes, service bulletins, data sheets, catalogs, brochures, correspondence, and elsewhere.

Special training seminars, "caravans" and field demonstration and instruction trailers, and special events are unusual but good channels for obtaining primary data. Material assembled for a trade show may be totally new or newly organized and may also have been thoroughly reviewed. Since these latter presentations combine showmanship and information, they may not only be superior sources for information, but may help in identifying the areas of greatest possible reader interest. The material will have already been formulated for simple presentation and will certainly have been designed to achieve maximum impact. Remember, writing an article for publication is an exercise in showmanship!

EVALUATING YOUR SOURCES

The value of the data and the sources is a matter for concern. What value can you place on a corporate annual report versus a monthly progress report? What value can you place on a published article that is used as a standard reference versus a paper or presentation that has been given more recently at an international technical convocation? You may find it difficult to locate what should be good data in secondary sources because poor data reside in the standard sources.

When you go to your various sources keep in mind that the accuracy of some data may be doubtful. Consider how the data have been interpreted in the past. How cautious has the company management been? Perhaps the facts are correct, but management has modified its interpretation of those facts to avoid legal problems. You may find that a document that gets high-level scrutiny contains less grandiose claims while one going to the engineering department contains broader claims.

Some sources contain data, claims, and interpretations that are less carefully scrutinized for accuracy than others. Information in an annual report may be more reliable than information in a sales presentation because more care will have been taken in its preparation. Use sources that have been carefully reviewed in preference to those that give raw data. Estimate the value of your sources in terms of the potential validity of the data as well as their completeness.

MINING THE GOLD

Some sources are mother lodes while others are dry holes (to mix a metaphor). A source may be potentially valuable but may be too difficult to tap or may impinge on an area where someone may take offense. When you seek information, it helps to set up an order of precedence based on your estimate of the difficulty of obtaining useful information and reaching helpful people.

If visits or interviews are difficult to arrange because of company or organization policy, physical plant layout, geographic distance, or security requirements, use sources that you can reach more easily by mail or telephone. You should never attempt to tap a source whose information cannot be published. Exceptions are when a source has essential background information that you need in order to understand the entire subject or when a source may help you locate other sources whose material is publishable. Determine your needs beforehand. Unless you do so, you may create unnecessary problems for yourself.

Once you have determined your objective (usually with the aid of a detailed outline), decide what specific types of data you need, go to the data sources, and get the information; don't linger. Take into account the time and cost required, the space you plan to devote to the information, the urgency of the need, the intended use of the data, and the likelihood of finding sufficiently complete and useful information. Evaluate your objectives and select the best way to proceed.

MINIMIZE YOUR COSTS

It is worth dwelling a bit longer on the matter of costs of collecting data. You will spend much more time assembling and reviewing data than writing the article. Data collection and review are time-intensive activities: that is, costly in terms of time. You might spend days or weeks just researching your data sources, then physically write the article in a very short time, perhaps only a few hours.

If some of the data are contained in very long documents, you will find yourself going through an incredible mass of paper to get at a few nuggets. Make your job easier. Once you have located what you want, copy the key items that you need so as to keep your pile of papers to a minimum. You can go back to the original source document if you later need to recheck some detail. If you can copy everything to the same size, you will have an easier time organizing your materials later.

INDEX YOUR MATERIALS

When you have a complete set of materials, index them item by item. Make a list and assign a reference number or letter to each different document. You may wish to assign subdesignations as well, if the material is very complex or has information you will not need. You will want to avoid having to review everything each time you refer to the document. Organize and collate your references and bibliography and type up this listing in an appropriate sequence. You can use this as a checklist for each document you will use when you start to write. How to work with these index numbers will be described in Chapter 8.

If you have a lot of material, you may want to place it in looseleaf binders. If this gets too voluminous, you may need file folders that can expand as you add material.

MORE DATA, MORE SOURCES

Table 1 lists 39 of the most important types of data or documentation that are useful for writers of business and professional articles. The table includes only items that would normally be found within a company or research organization. There are at least 100 other possible sources, some of which are so specialized that they are not normally available to most researchers. Among the sources are listed, for example, would be personnel bulletins to employees, statements to the press by corporate officers, overhaul manuals, and published material of a restricted or unique nature. If these sources are to be valuable at all, help will usually be needed in locating them. Once you start with the sources listed here, you will encounter people who may know of more arcane repositories of data.

TABLE 1. Some major data sources for business and professional articles.

Data Source	Reference Number
Advertisements	1
Annual reports (corporate)	2
Application notes	3
Audiovisual presentations	4
Blueprints	5
Brochure describing product and its uses	6
Catalog, full product line	7
Catalog, short form	8
Correspondence of all sorts	9
Data sheet or specification sheet	10
Development reports	11
Direct mail about new product or new application	12
Directories	13
Feasibility reports (engineering and marketing justification for undertaking work)	14
Feature article on applications of product	15
Feature article on experiences of users	16
Feature design article	17
Field service reports	18
House organ, engineering and scientific	19
House organ, general and customer-oriented	20
House organ, how-to and instructional	21
House organ, tutorial	22
How-to feature article	23
Instructional manual: operation and maintenance	24
Market research reports	25
Microfilm file	26
Models, displays, and demonstrations	27
New literature releases	28
New product releases	29
Personal interviews with customers, engineers, technicians, specialists, etc.	30
Price lists	31
Progress reports (monthly, quarterly, etc.)	32
Salesperson or engineering representative	33
Service and technical bulletins	34
Technical and management proposals	35
Technical notes	36
Technical papers and oral presentations	37
Trade shows and related materials	38
Training programs, internal and external	39

TABLE 2. Relative usefulness of the major data sources.

Section 1. Excellent Sources

If this is the information you want . . .	*Check these data sources*
Information to help select products and determine their availability:	
News of existing products	1, 3, 4, 6, 7, 8, 10, 12, 13, 20, 22, 26, 27, 33, 34, 38
Information on related products, to augment the value of existing products	1, 3, 4, 6, 9, 11, 12, 14, 20, 22, 27, 34, 36, 38
Technical specifications	3, 6, 7, 8, 10, 12, 15, 16, 22, 24, 26, 33, 34, 35, 36
Concept and design approach	4, 5, 9, 11, 12, 14, 17, 19, 24, 27, 30, 35, 37
Marketing objectives	9, 12, 14, 20, 25, 27, 30, 38
Application information needed to evaluate suitability of particular product for desired objectives:	
Performance specifications	6, 10, 11, 12, 23, 24, 29, 32, 33, 34, 35, 36, 39
Operational setups (including applications)	3, 6, 21, 22, 23, 24, 27, 35, 39
Operation and maintenance procedures	15, 23, 24
Installation data	5, 12, 21, 23, 24, 26, 32, 34
Availability and price	7, 8, 9, 10, 21, 28, 29, 31, 33, 38
Company's ability to produce and deliver on time	2, 4, 7, 9, 10, 21, 27, 31, 33, 38
Information on operation and use of the product:	
Qualitative data on product performance	3, 4, 6, 7, 10, 11, 16, 19, 22, 20, 37
Quantitative data on product performance	4, 7, 10, 11, 12, 15, 18, 19, 21, 22, 23, 24, 32, 35, 36, 37
Comparative evaluations of similar or related products	6, 9, 11, 33
Operating experiences of users	4, 9, 16, 18, 21, 25, 30, 33, 34, 37

Note that the designations given in the table may not be identical with terminology you are familiar with or will

Section 2. Good Sources

If this is the information you want . . .	Check these data sources
Information to help select products and determine their availability:	
News of existing products	2, 5, 28, 31
Information on related products, to augment the value of existing products	2, 13, 15, 19, 26, 29, 31, 33, 35, 37
Technical specifications	5, 11, 19, 32, 38
Concept and design approach	3, 6, 10, 15, 21, 25, 32, 36, 38, 39
Marketing objectives	3, 4, 16, 17, 19, 33, 35, 38
Application information needed to evaluate suitability of particular product for desired objectives:	
Performance specifications	3, 5, 7, 14, 15, 17, 19, 21, 22, 26, 27, 28
Operational setups (including applications)	5, 7, 11, 12, 15, 16, 17 18, 19, 32, 35, 37
Operation and maintenance procedures	3, 21, 27, 34
Installation data	3, 6, 7, 10, 15, 17, 18, 19, 22, 27
Availability and price	1, 6, 12, 26, 35
Company's ability to produce and deliver on time	8, 18, 25, 29, 30, 35
Information on operation and use of the product:	
Qualitative data on product performance	5, 8, 9, 12, 15, 17, 20, 23, 24, 33, 34, 39
Quantitative data on product performance	3, 5, 6, 8, 16, 17, 29, 30, 34
Comparative evaluations of similar or related products	3, 4, 10, 12, 15, 17, 19, 25, 27, 30, 34, 36, 37, 39
Operating experiences of users	6, 19, 20, 23

encounter. You will have to assess the titling and contents of documentation you work with to determine where the material may fall in this scheme.

Table 2 shows the relative usefulness of the various sources. The reference numbers correspond to the numbers in Table 1. To use this table properly, work first with Sections 1 and 4. This will lead you to your richest sources and keep you from the poorest

Section 3. Poor Sources

If this is the information you want . . .	*Check these data sources*
Information to help select products and determine their availability:	
News of existing products	9, 14, 16, 19, 21, 25, 29, 30, 36
Information on related products, to augment the value of existing products	5, 7, 10, 16, 21, 23, 24, 25, 28
Technical specifications	1, 4, 9, 13, 14, 20, 21, 23, 27, 28, 29, 31
Concept and design approach	7, 13, 16, 18, 20, 22, 23, 33, 34
Marketing objectives	1, 2, 5, 6, 11, 15, 32, 36, 39
Application information needed to evaluate suitability of particular product for desired objectives:	
Performance specifications	8, 9, 16, 18, 25
Operational setups (including applications)	8, 10, 26, 29, 33, 34, 38
Operation and maintenance procedures	6, 7, 12, 16, 18, 19, 22, 35, 36, 39
Installation data	8, 11, 33, 35, 36, 37, 38, 39
Availability and price	18, 30, 34
Company's ability to produce and deliver on time	6, 12, 16, 28, 34, 37
Information on operation and use of the product:	
Qualitative data on product performance	1, 2, 14, 18, 21, 25, 27, 29, 32, 35, 36
Quantitative data on product performance	1, 14, 20, 27, 33
Comparative evaluations of similar or related products	7, 16, 18, 20, 21, 22, 23, 29, 38
Operating experiences of users	1, 3, 15, 36, 39

ones, thereby reducing your searching time and effort. Note that the table is only a rough guide. Don't discount any source in advance; always keeps an open mind. You may find excellent material in documents that are cited in the table as unlikely locations. No two organizations generate and handle their data in precisely the same way. Often, personality plays a part in these

Section 4. Sources of No Likely Value

If this is the information you want . . .	Check these data sources
Information to help select products and determine their availability:	
News of existing products	11, 15, 17, 18, 23, 24, 32, 35, 36, 39
Information on related products, to augment the value of existing products	8, 17, 18, 30, 32, 39
Technical specifications	2, 17, 18, 25, 31, 37, 39
Concept and design approach	1, 2, 8, 26, 28, 29, 31
Marketing objectives	7, 8, 10, 13, 18, 21, 22, 23, 24, 26, 28, 29, 31, 33
Application information needed to evaluate suitability of particular product for desired objectives:	
Performance specifications	1, 2, 4, 13, 20, 30, 31, 37, 38
Operational setups (including applications)	1, 2, 4, 9, 13, 14, 20, 25, 28, 30, 31
Operation and maintenance procedures	1, 2, 4, 5, 8, 9, 10, 11, 13, 14, 17, 20, 25, 26, 28, 29, 30, 31, 32, 33, 37, 38
Installation data	1, 2, 4, 9, 13, 14, 16, 20, 25, 28, 29, 30, 31
Availability and price	2, 3, 4, 5, 11, 13, 14, 15, 16, 17, 19, 20, 22, 23, 24, 25, 27, 32, 36, 37, 39
Company's ability to produce and deliver on time	1, 3, 5, 11, 13, 14, 15, 17, 19, 20, 22, 23, 24, 26, 32, 36, 39
Information on operation and use of the product:	
Qualitative data on product performance	13, 26, 28, 31, 38
Quantitative data on product performance	2, 9, 13, 25, 26, 28, 31, 38, 39
Comparative evaluations of similar or related products	1, 2, 5, 8, 13, 14, 24, 26, 28, 31, 32, 35
Operating experiences of users	2, 5, 7, 8, 10, 11, 12, 13, 14, 17, 22, 24, 26, 27, 28, 29, 31, 32, 35, 38

differences. If the original author of a document felt that he needed certain background information, his document may turn out to be the best source for a particular type of data, whereas you could not expect to find such similarly titled documentation in other companies.

You will need to know the nature of the company's business or the work done by an organization or society, to learn about its documentation resources. For instance, a company that does most of its business with the government will not possess a catalog. A company that does no business with the government may generate no technical proposals.

Some sources are likely to be unreliable. Sales personnel are notoriously undereducated in the business of their companies. That they sell anything at all is sometimes a compliment more to their perseverance, enthusiasm, and tenacity than to their knowledge. Nevertheless, a salesperson may come along who is better informed than even the designers and engineers. His information is likely to be quite good; it can and probably should be used. You will sense how valid his data are when you speak to him. You may also be directed to a knowledgeable individual by others who respect his expertise.

Note that in Table 2, all information has been placed on an equal footing in terms of accuracy and validity. There are many instances in which documentation is not written in accordance with good practice; for example, a new product release fails to mention the name of the product, blueprints lack dimensions, and so forth.

As you go through your source materials you will find that there is considerable overlap of data among documents. This is a decided advantage, for should you find that you cannot obtain access to a primary source you may be able to locate all or most of what you seek in a more accessible secondary source. Table 2 shows you where this is most likely to occur.

THE THEORY OF INFORMATIONAL HIERARCHY

Some commentators on writing see information sources as forming a hierarchy, with documents higher in the hierarchy developed only from those below. In this view, sources on the lowest level might be called "documentation" while those on the highest are attuned to sales and marketing. This theory assumes that no new information seeps into the system; only interpretations can be added.

This is often, but not always, a true picture. Sometimes a less technical presentation contains data suitable for use in a more technical one. The extent to which data are modified in the progression from most technical to most marketing in orientation varies widely. Marketing-oriented materials may contain newer data because they were prepared after the research was performed and therefore reflect later developments. Don't operate on the basis of the hierarchy theory. It is only a theory and does not always apply in practice.

Be selective, researching in accordance with your needs. Don't assume that any particular source will not work for you. As an example, some sales material is highly reliable because it is developed directly from prototypes. Data contained in the sales department are often more easily obtained than the same data appearing in an internal technical report. Technical material is often given to the sales staff at the direction of the corporate management and is revised and verified for ease of presentation. You should have no trouble getting that material since you will probably be working for corporate management or for the sales or marketing department.

One very valuable yet frequently overlooked source of information is correspondence with customers and potential customers. When a product, service, or system is under development, there tends to be a high proportion of customer input. Such correspondence frequently is useful in tracking down data concerning the developmental stages of a project. Early correspondence may establish one of the most important parts of your article: the justification for undertaking the project. Since most articles are written with the knowledge (and often at the direction) of the sales department, these letters are among the easiest materials to obtain.

Don't assume that because you work in one area you cannot

get data from another area. Don't accept the word of anyone else that the document you're looking for is useless or is not where you hope to find it. No one can get into your mind to know what you are really looking for or how it may help you, nor can they evaluate data that neither you nor they have yet seen.

When you work, start from wherever you happen to be. It is not necessary to obtain your data in any particular sequence; you will develop a plan after you have begun to see patterns develop. Then you will fill in as you develop your ideas and learn where to look.

GET COOPERATION

Too many times, authors believe that they can get all the information they require simply because they want it or because higher management wants them to get it. This is seldom the case. You generally need the cooperation of others to obtain data. Even when management has given you carte blanche, you cannot step on toes. Management may choose to kill the project rather than see people in its organization upset.

If you think there is any chance of such sensitivity, don't proceed to a specified source of data on your own. Rather, get the cooperation of those people who are likely to have access to the data. This is particularly important when the information is known to reside in only one location. If possible, get assistance from several people. They may have complementary data that have not heretofore been combined in the manner you are planning to present them in.

The people you approach will often help you to find more materials and avoid ambiguities or sources about which there is some question. Sometimes they will ask to review the material before giving it to you. Grant them this opportunity, as well as later letting them review your finished article. Although they probably will not comment on portions other than those concerning their special interest, they may make suggestions that will improve your paper. Such people are really data sources in themselves. You are tapping knowledge they possess that has not been committed to written form. Be considerate of their requests; failure to do so may preclude working with them in the future.

ASK THE EDITOR

If you have difficulty finding some data and you have already queried the editor and know that he is interested in the article, get him involved in the search. You may be surprised at how much he knows about your subject matter, even if he is not conversant with the technical details. You may also be surprised at the people he has access to, whom you cannot get to see without his help.

Sometimes the editor will suggest impartial people whom he feels may be able to help. Some of these people will want to receive credit, some will be willing to forgo credit, and some will insist on anonymity. In any case, by citing impartial sources you can greatly enhance the credibility and validity of your presentation.

Remember, too, that the editor is going to be involved with the article at some later stage. Get him involved and committed early. He will then have a personal stake in seeing that your article is published in his journal.

8

---

organizing your presentation

SOME PEOPLE advise potential writers to "just tell a story," writing as they speak. This approach is simplistic and will bring almost certain failure. It is true that the vocabulary and grammatical phrasings used in English speech are easily translated into writing. However, the similarities tend to stop there.

When instructed to "tell a story" the writer begins at the beginning and ends at the end, in temporal terms. This, as suitable as it may be in a social milieu, simply will not work in a business or professional article. In a face-to-face encounter the audience is already conditioned to listen to the storyteller. Even if the audience is not receptive, common courtesy enables the teller to proceed to his conclusion. No such good fortune greets the writer.

The writer must always seek to capture the attention of the reader and keep him interested until the article ends. When he does this successfully he has done his writing well. Often it is style that will keep the reader interested, not subject matter. It was the subject matter that attracted him in the first place. Now the objective is to keep him interested.

In professional journals, most articles are expected to be

written in accordance with styles and standards that have been found most useful by the particular professional community. They are presented in the manner most customarily used in the scientific or technical discipline, even to the use of certain technical jargon.

No such rigorous requirements exist for most business publications. The approach in a general business magazine is different from the approach used in a professional journal. Both types of journals consider the educational attainments and professional experience of their respective audiences, but the similarities end there. The editor of a professional journal is normally bound by very rigid rules and often has a committee to report to. The editor of a business journal, because of the commercial bent of the business press, is free to make arbritrary changes in style and requirements. He heads his own "business," so to speak, and runs it as he wishes.

The business journal editor is a practitioner of an inexact science. He is obligated to transmit facts within the rules of proper grammar, but beyond that there is little he does that can be judged as the "right" way or the only way to communicate clearly. Two editors may carry out the same project using different approaches, methods, and styles. Each would be correct, though there would be considerable differences in the end products.

OUTLINING

Organizing and outlining your presentation is probably the most important part of your entire writing activity. Some authorities believe that it comprises more than half the work. When you have drawn up your outline, even before you have verified your data, you may be more than half finished with the entire project.

Any article that is to run more than a thousand words should be outlined. If this sounds like elementary school advice, it is worth following. An outline does not have to be a rigorous

Harvard-style outline. Since it will probably be only for your personal use it can be as rough or as finished as you require. If more than one person is to work on the article a formal written outline will be more than merely helpful; it will prevent omissions of content.

An outline helps you to organize not only your presentation but your source materials as well. Through an outline you will discover whether you have assembled all the data you need and whether the material you have collected is adequate in depth and scope. It may be helpful to start your outline before you complete your search for data. You will have to do some research, however (or know your subject sufficiently), before you can formulate any semblance of an outline and before you can even ask the right questions.

For an article for the business or professional press the outline not only provides you with a road map for your work but can help your editor. He may be able to guide you to changes, sources, and ideas you may have overlooked, perhaps even picking up a portion of the outline and filling in an area inaccessible to you.

Expect to modify your outline as you go along. You will find yourself reevaluating the quality of your data. You will change your mind about the importance of some of the information you felt strongly about earlier. And you will certainly upgrade some points, change the emphasis on various points, and so forth.

You will have already indexed your source material, as discussed in Chapter 7, so each item will have a number or letter. You now use these index numbers in your outline. Beside each item in the outline place the index number or numbers of appropriate reference materials. One item on your outline may carry three or four index numbers; another item may carry only one. This procedure will help you when you start to write. As you prepare each section of the article you will need to keep available for reference only those data sources which apply to that section.

As you outline and index your sources you will ascertain whether you have collected all the data you think you will need. You may learn of the existence of some material that might be useful to you. If you can get to it easily it is worthwhile to seek it out. Don't assume that you will be able to anticipate all your needs when outlining. Some may be discovered only as you are actually writing.

For every item of your outline, you should have at least one highly reputable source or two sources of a slightly lower caliber. If you cannot locate a source for your item, you may have to modify your outline. If you do not (or cannot) change the outline you will find it necessary to seek secondary data sources.

When your outline is complete you will find that you have cross-referenced all your data to your outline and vice versa.

Once you have a solid outline you are in business. You will have established your objectives, will know what data you need, will know the approximate length of your article, and will be able to anticipate troublesome areas and begin to cope with them. An outline is somewhat like a paint-by-numbers set or a crossword puzzle. You have little room to go wrong. The proper things to do are prescribed, and everything else is proscribed.

With this type of system you will also find that you can write various sections of the article as separate units. You may be able to proceed in any sequence you want rather than writing in the order in which the final article will appear. You might write the conclusion first, then an explanation of an early graph, and so on. You can leave the tough parts for last, after you have thoroughly digested all the available data.

LENGTH VS. IMPORTANCE

Plan each portion of the article in accordance with its importance. If an idea is quite significant, plan to give it extensive treatment. If it is relatively unimportant, try to gloss over it even if you feel you would need much space to explain it fully. When you don't feel it is worth drawing the reader's attention to a point, write in a way that will cause him to pass over it lightly.

A balance of space is just as important as a balance of sentence structure. If you know that you may have difficulty making an important point, cover the requisite space then plan graphics to go with it. It is the total space that will count. The reader will spend as much time on an illustration as he will on text that occupies the same physical space.

PLAN YOUR ILLUSTRATIONS

When you work up your outline, plan your illustrations right along with the text. You might find that you have better pictures than words. You will certainly find that some ideas cannot be expressed in words; only a picture will do. It is obviously ridiculous to spend time describing a chart when you can show the chart itself. Likewise with comparative performance curves, and so forth.

Index your illustrations when you wish to use visual materials that have appeared in reference data. Place these index numbers right on the outline, along with the index references for textual material. You will save a lot of searching later.

Photographs and other visuals may not exist when you outline. If you know that you will need illustrations, plan for them. List the subject matter for artwork and even plan the angles for photographs that you want taken. Be specific. You may have to transmit these concepts to a photographer who will have no idea what you are talking about until he gets to the shooting location, and perhaps not even then. Leave as little to chance as possible. The more specifically you outline your illustrations the more accurate they will be and the more likely it is that they will come out the way you planned them.

GET THEIR ATTENTION

An article in a business or professional journal is similar to a newspaper story, although the event being reported on may be of less immediate interest and less spectacular. At no time is the reader "captive" to the writer or to the journal. He can put down the magazine any time he loses interest, his telephone rings, his children call, he gets warm, he gets cold, or the subject seems too simple or too complex. No coercive force obligates him to continue to read something in which he no longer has an interest.

If the headline and introductory material (abstract, editor's note, subhead, etc.) indicate that the subject matter of the article may be of interest to him he will probably start reading it. (In a professional journal the abstract has to appeal to him.) If he reads beyond the second paragraph he will generally read at least halfway through the article. If he does not read beyond the first paragraph he will never read the article.

Today's reader, whether businessperson or engineer, is an individual who is hurried. He has little time to waste. Information that can be gotten from a reference book or textbook should be left in the library to be sought out at his convenience. What readers want from a magazine is news, and they want it fast. They also want to know "What's in it for me?"

This impatience on the part of readers is the reason newspaper reporters use the five "W"s and the "H" (who, what, where when, why, and how) and put most or all of them in the lead paragraph. For the business and professional magazine this approach is not necessary and often is not desirable. Since the business reader is interested in obtaining information, he expects material to be presented in an unemotional fashion. Excitement in the first paragraph is not nearly as important as a promise of value to come.

Note that business articles tend to have different types of openings from professional articles. The business article should very quickly tell the reader what is of greatest interest to him: the conclusions. The professional article will very quickly tell the reader what is of greatest interest to him: the point from which the newly disclosed knowledge had commenced.

The reader of a professional journal generally has technical knowledge concerning the subject matter that is equal to that of the writer. This is certainly not the case with a business journal.

Articles in professional journals have a strong flavor of documentation, while those in business magazines generally are written to impart information that is not readily available to the reader from other sources.

Since the approaches of professional journals and business magazines usually differ, the two approaches will be treated separately in this chapter. The divergence, however, should not be considered absolute. Sometimes an article in a professional journal will disclose results of work that would otherwise not have come to the attention of the reader. Sometimes an article in a business magazine will be technical and documentary in nature.

Given these conditions the writer of a professional article that is designed to appear in a business magazine should approach his material as if he is speaking to co-equal colleagues. For the business articles in the professional journal a "business" approach is appropriate.

CONVERTING ORAL TO WRITTEN FORM

When you are working with a paper that has already been delivered in oral form there is still a need to organize or reorganize the material to suit the written format. As will be seen later, certain styles are expected by the readers of certain types of articles. You may have to modify your material to the appropriate acceptable written style.

An article can sometimes be published unchanged in form from a paper that was delivered orally. Unless the paper is truly a fascinating piece of writing the average reader will not go through the entire article in the hope of finding treasure at the end of his search. More likely, unless he can foresee a promise to be fulfilled, he will stop reading.

Generally, conversion from oral to written form involves reducing the didactic tone, moving from oratory to discourse, and changing the sequence of presentation. Because the English language does not require a change of grammatical structure for the change in audience this transition is not too difficult.

THE BUSINESS ARTICLE: CONCLUSIONS COME FIRST

The writer of the business article should state his conclusions at the outset. He will be more likely to capture readers with this approach than with any other. He shows the reader why it is important for him to continue to read: that is, offers him a promise of value to come.

It is appropriate for the writer of a business article to give his own evaluations of his work. He is, it is assumed, an expert in his field and one whose opinion is respected. In some cases he may qualify his conclusions so the claims he makes are not too grandiose. At times the actual writer is a ghostwriter, such as a public relations specialist, who is being paid for his writing by a corporation. This does not necessitate any change in the basic approach but may influence the tone of the presentation.

A summary paragraph may follow the conclusions, or, if appropriate, may be used as a lead paragraph. In the latter case the summary paragraph is much like the lead paragraph of a newspaper story. A great deal of information, without documentation or explanation, is crowded into the paragraph. The proof follows as the story devolves.

You should seldom attempt to draw conclusions or give a summary of information that is not drawn from the substance of the article. Many authors fall into this trap, but it is unwise to make statements that cannot be documented, even when there seem to be valid technical or other reasons for doing so. This approach may be acceptable if documentation is cited, but it is better actually to produce the evidence in the article itself.

THE PROFESSIONAL ARTICLE: THE PAST COMES FIRST

Since professional articles—also called papers—are directed to readers whose knowledge of the subject matter is equal to that of the writer, the reader is likely to respond best to an opening that tells him the starting point of the work reported on. The point of departure is needed in order to establish the validity of the work. If the lead paragraph promises to relate a story of a new development that has arisen from a previously known and accepted edge of the state of the art, the reader will be intrigued and will continue to read. A work that is based on obsolete foundations would probably not hold the reader's interest, if, in fact, the editor or review board would accept such material.

The reader of the professional article is quite capable of following the work as its development is unfolded. When he reaches the end he will form his own conclusions. For many authors this is the most frustrating aspect of writing such articles; the reader draws different conclusions from the same evidence.

AN ARTICLE IS NOT A LAB REPORT

To approach an article as if it were a report is not appropriate. In this "lab report" type of writing, a summary of basic conditions is given, the equipment and materials are described, the process is discussed, and conclusions are drawn. Sometimes a summary is included. Most readers will comprehend material that is presented in this matter, but the approach does not make interesting reading. It is dull and pedantic.

An article should contain a summary of results, not the results themselves. Detailed documentation, if needed, should be provided only in footnotes and references.

Cover the justification early in the writing: the question of why such research efforts were undertaken in the first place. By using this approach you answer the reader's primary question: "Why should I bother to read this article?" The reader always wants to know "What's in it for me?"

First, the lead paragraphs should promise the reader that the article contains information he will find of value. Second, is there a new product, a new process, or a new concept that could be useful, informative, valuable, or profitable to know about? If such a promise is held up to the reader and kept before him constantly throughout the article, he is most likely to read to the end.

At some point in the article the reader may discover that the promise you have held out to him is one he cannot foresee attaining or one he would probably not be able to employ. He will therefore stop reading. If a particular reader does see the prospect of a pot of informational gold at the end of the rainbow he will continue reading. People do read business and professional publications in search of the proverbial gold. These magazines are in business primarily to inform, not entertain. There must be a promise of a fairly concrete reward for the reader who threads his way through an entire issue.

PROCEEDING THROUGH THE "W"s

Following your opening, you should proceed logically through the rest of the "W"s. You have already given the "why," so now you will, in some logical fashion, go through the "what," "where," "when," and "who." These data validate your work. For instance, telling which companies or individuals have been involved in the project provides a testimonial as effective as a testimonial of a friend whose judgment you trust in the selection of books, movies, or restaurants. If the description involves a highly respected company or researcher, the reader will probably know this.

The "where" and "when" are needed to complete the tale and to place the data in proper perspective. Without such information, the reader has no knowledge of the currency of your material. He may presuppose the existence of data which are not valid.

LEAVE "HOW" FOR LAST

Generally it is best to leave "how" for last. Since most readers are not likely to duplicate the work reported on, they need only a summary of procedures. Sometimes the article is itself about a procedure. But even an article on procedures should be structured so the minuscule details are left for last or, preferably, left out entirely.

The business article often ends with procedural details. The professional article may end with such details, with an author's summary or conclusions, or with both. If the article contains a forecast—that is, a best guess of the future value of the work described—this belongs at the end. When a forecast is the entire subject of an article the most logical ordering is a conclusion and summary, an exposition, and then a discussion of the working tools.

WHEN TO BREAK THE RULES

Only the most skilled and experienced writer should attempt to break the rules. He will be someone who has done his marketing evaluation and knows his audience thoroughly. He will generally be a staff writer or a person who is so well known in the field that whatever he writes will be read simply because of his reputation. The occasional writer should not break the rules, at risk of losing the value of his creation.

If the organizational guidelines set forth in this chapter are followed the acceptability of any article will be enhanced considerably. The editor would have to do little or no reorganizing of your material. A magazine editor seldom minds doing minimal editing for style, spelling, abbreviations, and so forth. Problems in organization are major and either will require considerable work or will lead to rejection.

AN ARTICLE IS NOT A BOOK

Bear in mind that an article is different from a book. Just as a book is generally not a group of articles strung together to form an integrated whole, an article is generally not a piece of a more comprehensive written work. Your article must be organized in a way that provides completeness within the framework of the few thousand words and several illustrations that you use. You will not have time, nor will the reader have patience, for you to build up to a grand climax. Most articles start with the climax and then work down to the nitty-gritty data relating to justification and application. If you follow the organizational style of a book in writing an article you will often find that the head is at the tail and the tail is somewhere in the middle.

You may want to leave the reader with some impact if he stays with you to the end. This is fine if such a luxury is available to you. The impact that you intend to achieve at the end should not be taken from elsewhere. It should be superflous because most readers will never get that far.

A book is read under different circumstances than a business or professional publication. Your article must stand by itself. It is a complete story and will be read without any connection with other material. As a writer, you are a craftsman (or craftswoman) who is called in to perform a task and then leave. The resulting product—the article—will presumably be perfect and complete.

9

---

research and
documentation

In Chapter 7 we discussed how to evaluate the available data sources. Once you have begun to locate your data, you must be selective in order to obtain the full benefit from them.

You will, of course, first have to read your material. Read initially in a cursory manner, culling out whatever is unlikely to be useful. Review the remaining data and classify them according to their value to you. By doing this you will establish your best sources first; you may not have to go through your secondary sources. This can save you time and effort.

You will be concerned with the professional standing that any of your references enjoy in the professional community. You will feel more secure quoting from a highly regarded source than one which has been the subject of controversy. Certainly you will not want to work with a reference that has been discredited, unless you want to cite it for purposes of balance or it contains valuable background material. If you have doubts, just leave the citation off your list of references.

Prepare to be quite specific in your references. You should be able to produce copies of such material, particularly the questionable ones. Pay special attention to revisions and make certain you actually use the editions you cite.

"Best available technology" is a phrase that has been applied widely in the sciences and business. This is a suitable guide to use in your research and documentation. It is a limiting concept; restrict yourself to only what you actually need for your article. Otherwise you will find yourself collecting enough data for a book with nowhere to get it published.

YOU ARE THE AUTHORITY

The difference between an expert and an authority is that an expert fully knows his subject while an authority is someone whom everybody believes knows his subject. When you write, you may or may not be an expert; you are always regarded as an authority. You can enjoy the advantages that this situation confers on you.

If you are reporting on your own work (whether as an originator or surrogate writer) you are the expert. No one will dispute your claim to expertise. You are not disqualified as an expert because your ideas are unconventional. If there is a dispute, you are just one expert with whom other experts do not happen to agree. (And you have probably known that all along.)

A common mistake of many authors, especially those who report on their own work, is to try to be infallible. It is not worth the trouble. Nobody is infallible, especially with an article. An article is not a major publication and should not be accorded the time or effort required for a book or a formal report. This is the reason some professional associations have review committees to pass on the suitability of materials before allowing them to be published in the associations' journals. This is why editors read your material. This may even be why readers overlook errors; they are really so easy to find.

Errors of fact are serious, typographic errors usually less so. It is not always possible to know whether a mistake was a typographical error or resulted from poor reporting on the part of the writer.

You have something to offer the reader. You bring your special knowledge, but you should be able to back it up. If you have not done your research task completely you will fail to convince your reader. The editor may accept an article about an improperly researched project, either because he is not truly conversant with the details of your subject matter or because he welcomes the possibility of some controversy to stimulate reader interest. You will not, however, gain the type of favorable reception that the work of writing an article deserves. So, plan your research to be complete: complete, that is, within a predetermined scope.

ASK THE EDITOR ABOUT SCOPE

Limit the scope of your article by covering only material that is provable, that can be documented, and that will leave you with a completed article that is neither too long nor too short. This will minimize the effort spent on the research for the article itself and relieve you of much superfluous, time-consuming, and tedious work.

If you have any doubts about scope, ask your editor for advice. He will have an excellent feel for the audience you are writing for and will know the depth of coverage you should go to. However, this should not necessarily serve to limit the scope of your research; you may have to go further. He may, for example, ask you to limit yourself to highlights only.

After talking with your editor you may find you have already done all the research you need to do or may find you have done far too little. Frequently an author believes he has completed his work only to find that the editor has understood the objectives differently, visualizing a different slant for the article, and the entire job has to be done over. You may decide it isn't worth doing over and discontinue work on the article. At least you will know this before you go any further.

If your article is scheduled to be reviewed by an editorial board your editor can certainly guide you to a proper research and writing approach. He knows what the review committee will consider important, what it may let pass without much comment, and what may cause it to disqualify the article. Your editor can also misjudge. Plan to work well above a minimum acceptable level.

BE ABLE TO ANSWER LOGICAL QUESTIONS

You should be able to answer any logical questions of fact or source data that are likely to arise in the reader's mind. If you have chosen your sources and data well, this will be easy enough. If not, you'll sweat it out.

No single article ever contains complete documentation on a topic. A reader who wants to know more will go to other articles or documentation. Many of these data sources will be ones that you supposedly drew on when researching your article. You may have quoted or paraphrased them as necessary.

Some questions that may arise may be so technical that you may not be the person best qualified to supply the answers. You should know who would be qualified.

If you are writing for a team of experts, whether as a technical writer or as a participant on the team, you may not have personal knowledge adequate to answer all questions. You need to know which individuals can answer which questions. The editor will expect you to transmit their knowledge to a potential inquiring reader. You are the editor's communications link with the experts.

The editor will ask questions about facts, presentation form, and sources. He may be quite astute at finding factual inconsistencies. If the problems he identifies are true inconsistencies rather than the result of ambiguous writing you must go back to your original sources.

KEEP THE DOCUMENTATION AVAILABLE

As discussed in Chapter 7, you will have copies of the documents you will need, copied from the sources. Each item will be cross-indexed to its source with such information as journal, book, date, and location. You probably won't ever have to produce the copies, except possibly for people within your own organization. You will, however, have occasion to go back to them, so keep them handy. This will enable you to answer questions faster. Usually you will just have to keep your working materials intact until the article is published, unless you wish to hold onto them for another purpose (such as a follow-up article).

Make certain you clearly indicate which item is from which source. Think, for example, of what confusion would be created if you had two editions of the same book and there were changes from the earlier to the later edition that affected your quotations or data, and you failed to designate which edition the copies were from.

If you have filed your source materials in a logical way, cross-indexed them to your outline or on a copy of the completed manuscript, you should have no difficulty determining which materials support which points you have made.

Be prepared to include footnotes, references, a bibliography, and other conventional documentation if this is standard practice in your industry, your profession, the journal you want to publish in, or the type of article you are writing. I doubt that there is any business magazine editor who will refuse to publish an article because it cites secondary references. Many prefer such citations because they give an aura of competence, of "science."

REGARD THE EDITOR AS AN EXPERT

As far as you are concerned, the editor is always an expert. Sometimes he actually is one. He may be a Ph.D. in a field that has many Ph.D.'s, or may have spent 15 or 20 years in the industry and knows a great deal about it intuitively. Much more often, however, he is not an expert. But you will gain nothing by presuming he is not. He may have established such a fine reputation that nobody really knows whether he is or is not an expert, including himself.

The editor will know if you have done your research well. He will know enough about your field to question statements that seem odd, especially when your article deals with a subject familiar to most readers. If you are reporting on some arcane phase of a narrow technology, he will not usually be competent to judge your research but will be competent to judge the manner in which you report on it. He is usually competent to judge how well you correlate your material with other work in the field.

THE EDITOR MAY CALL ON EXPERTS

When the editor knows he does not have sufficient expertise to judge your work he may call on experts in the area. This generally will not happen when a review committee has to approve all articles that appear in the journal. It happens more with business magazines than with professional journals.

If the editor senses that something is not quite right yet is not sure it is quite wrong he may want to get another opinion about your material before proceeding to print. He may or may not notify you of his intention. You may find your material rejected after it is written because the reviewer identified items that showed that you did not make a strong enough case for your point of view. You might never know the real reason for a rejection. You do have the right to ask the editor, but don't ask him to put his reasons in writing. He may have to be less than honest with you if his words are to be committed to paper. Don't force him to spell out his objections. If you do you may put him in a position where he'll have to cut himself off from additional articles from you in the future.

CONTINUING WORK

Why stop at just one article? You may find that some of the research materials you have collected can be used to generate more articles. Don't keep so much that you overflow your filing space, but hold on to items that you know may not be easy to obtain later. Just as you would use leftover wallpaper to paper a closet rather than buying more wallpaper, you should make maximum use of the materials you have collected.

The items you keep may generate a technical letter, may be turned into an application story if your original article was a report on a major technical development, and so forth. You may find that when you assembled your data for your original article you already did much of the work toward a second, third, or even fourth article.

Authors of books, particularly when they have to do a lot of research, very often have material left over that they find suitable for articles and papers on narrower topics. You can do the same. Allow for this flexibility.

BUILDING A PERMANENT REFERENCE FILE

Many writers, particularly public relations consultants and corporate personnel who are handling technical public relations, build up permanent reference files. If you are a free-lance writer who is a specialist in a field you may also wish to do this.

There is no easy way to build a file. Materials come to you in no logical sequence. Often a good item is so deeply buried in a document that it is hard to know what value to place on the entire document. It is usually hard to categorize material unless you have had enough experience to know what patterns exist. The task of categorizing is especially difficult when you are just starting your file.

To start building a reference file, establish some main categories that you believe most of your material will fall into. As each of these files builds up you will learn which categories are too broad and must be regrouped into several, more limited categories. Gradually you will establish virtually all the major classifications you will be working with over a long period of time.

Don't attempt to set up a cross-filing system. Such a system is time-consuming at the outset, will require too much maintenance time, and rapidly becomes unwieldy.

Duplicate Detailed Data

Many documents contain data that are of real value in a number of areas. An annual report, for instance, contains policy information about many different aspects of company business. But a complete copy of the report does not need to be placed in each and every applicable category. It is sufficient to copy certain pages or to obtain several copies of the report and cut them up, then distribute the pages in the appropriate places in the file. Make sure every piece of paper carries a reference number or some other form of identification, so the material can be cited without the need to go to another source to find out what you already have in your possession. Proper notations can save you a lot of time when you are trying to maintain a train of thought when writing.

If you expect to have many documents that contain a variety of data, such as technical manuals, keep a separate master file of the complete documents. When setting up your master file study each document to determine which categories in the general file it may pertain to. Then write these categories (or key words designating the categories) on the document. When you are working with a specific classification you will have available the master documents that contain relevant data.

Depending on the size of your file you may work with anything from a few loose-leaf binders to a row of steel filing cabinets. Whatever the size of your file, it will not be easy to find everything germane to an article you are working on. There is a good possibility you will have to compromise. This is a type of compromise that editors and reviewers will generally accept. Some limitations are not easy to overcome and are not worth trying to overcome.

Keep the File Up to Date

Keeping your permanent file up to date is difficult at best and more likely impossible. You are generally so busy researching and writing that you have little time for the niceties of housekeeping. Yet some updating is essential—and really not so impossible after all.

Whenever you place new material in the file, review your old material on the topic and throw it out if the new document is comparable. Replace old brochures with newer ones. Even if an old brochure has some information the new one does not, you probably won't need it; information of value will show up in another source document. What you gain by keeping the old material does not compensate for the problems this will create when you start to work on a new writing project. Keep your material current.

On the other hand, don't discard material simply because it is old. It may not be obsolete. There may be a good reason why a new document has not been issued.

Keep Each Category Small

Try to keep only a limited number of documents in any single category. When you develop your classification system you will be tempted to have as few categories as possible. This becomes cumbersome when you find you must then go through many documents to get the data you seek. If you have more than 15 or 20 documents in a single category you have too few categories. You probably will not need to refer to all these materials as source data for any single article.

Most good articles, except roundup articles, require fewer than 10 documents. Even with a lengthy series of articles—say, seven articles that draw on 100 documents—you are unlikely to refer to more than 10 items per article (though some items not cited may be needed for background information). Even the figure of 100 is unrealistically large. It is more than most people need to write very technical books and higher than the average cited for Ph.D. dissertations.

What to Put into the File

Anything that is available in print is suitable material for your permanent file. All the materials cited in Table 1 in Chapter 7 are suitable. Other materials not noted may also be suitable if they contain information you may need. Tape recordings, audiovisual materials, slides, and overhead projection charts might also be included if they contain data not available in a more convenient form.

If you find that you draw upon a few documents repeatedly, transfer those documents into a master file, as discussed earlier. Keep your file small and concise and it will serve you well.

Your general file is not a good place to keep original artwork. Manuscripts, likewise, should not be placed in the reference file. If you have to refer to your file frequently, the material will age and deteriorate rapidly.

A File of Illustrations

Of course, you will want to keep the originals of your illustrations in a safe place. Set up a separate reference file for photographs, artwork, and other illustrations. This means that you have two files, one which has the originals of your illustrations and one which has copies.

Include only copies, not originals of your illustrations with your reference materials in the general file, putting them in the same file folders or loose-leaf binders you keep your other material in. If the original artwork is large and you cannot get copies small enough to fit into your file, copy a portion of the artwork and identify it in some way (e.g., with a blueprint number or acquisition number). Then fold it to fit. Just be sure to include copies. If you don't, you later may not know that you have existing art and may even abandon a project because of the cost of recreating this artwork.

Use whatever means of identification suits you best. Most photographs, for example, have some reference numbers assigned by the photographer. If you use these numbers the photographer has the responsibility to keep track of the negatives in this way as long as you are a customer.

Mounted artwork requires safe storage. If you do not have responsibility for safekeeping such material use the file system of those who do. If you do have this responsibility keep as little of the material as possible and keep that in large groupings so you can minimize your individual cross-references. If, for instance, you have all the artwork for a particular instruction manual, keep it all together. Don't remove pieces as you need them; duplicate them. Make reproducible copies. It will cost only a few cents per copy but will save you frustration and possibly a much greater expense if you cannot locate the original material when you need it later.

Date Your Materials

Date your reference materials when you get them. This point seems so obvious and trivial that it is often overlooked. A dating system is vital. It indicates which material you received earlier and which later. It may be able to tell you which material is older, which is more current, which you are more likely to find useful. It may enable you to locate the author. He might still be around if the material is recent; he may not be around if the material is old.

Photographs and blueprints are less frequently dated than printed material, but dates are essential for these items. Printed material may carry dates—not always in a straightforward manner, but capable of being interpreted.

Even if printed matter is dated, you may still need to date your material when you receive it. Many data sheets and other technical materials (brochures, manuals, proposals, etc.) have numbering systems that include a date. For instance, a number such as 577-ED might be the code for 5,000 copies produced by Educational Printers in 1977.

Your Reference File Isn't a Lending Library

You may not be working alone, but your files are yours alone or belong to your department. Keep them that way. Your reference file is not a lending library. If you think it is you will soon learn to your dismay that that which is lent is lost. It never comes back.

You are not a librarian, and you will have neither time nor

inclination to set up a lending system with all its checks. Since libraries, which have all sorts of protective systems, lose up to 10 percent of their materials every year, what chance do you have of keeping tabs on your material once it is out of your hands?

Top-level managers have a habit of requesting material. You cannot refuse them—or so you think. Actually you can and should refuse them access to your files. When they want something get it for them yourself. Then, either make certain the material they borrow is returned within a day or so or ask that they give you time to copy the material so they can work with it at their leisure. You will find them remarkably amenable to your suggestions and sympathetic to your problem of keeping your files intact. Convey to them that if they do not return your material or you do not make copies for them there is a chance they will never be able to obtain the material again. They will respect your wish to protect valuable materials.

Reference files should be made available only to the few people who depend on them. Keep strict control over your files. If people have unlimited access to them they will find ways of pilfering the materials without your knowledge. Don't be the nice guy. In this circumstance, nice guys finish last.

10

---

matters of style

THIS BOOK, as noted earlier, does not include any lessons in English grammar. But the way you write can affect your ability to communicate—and the main purpose of article writing is communication, not documentation, not the generation of data, not publicity, not anything else. If you do not communicate, you will have no reason to write because you will not be understood.

Use of colloquial English is generally quite acceptable. It may actually be preferable to the King's English. Jargon, on the other hand, is often unsuitable because many readers are not sufficiently knowledgeable in the technology to understand it. Also, in some industries, trade terms differ in various parts of the country. Worse yet, if the publication is one that has a large overseas readership, use of jargon may make your article totally incomprehensible.

COMMUNICATION IS THE NAME OF THE GAME

The reader does not read your material because you have written it. He is seeking information. If you want him to read your material, you must be clear and direct.

Your writing style should be such that your reader does not think about it consciously. It should not intrude on his thinking or misdirect him so he believes he is reading for literary value when he really wants to know what you are saying. Remember the announcer at the railroad station who, in stentorian tones, broadcast the station stops with the final words: "and all points west." All anyone ever heard or remembered was "and all points west." The mode of presentation caused the message to be lost.

To communicate most effectively, meet the expectations of the reader. If he is likely to prefer long sentences, give him long sentences. If he is less literate, allow for shorter sentences and simpler sentence structures. If he is especially literate, he will have no difficulty comprehending material that is replete with polysyllabic words and complex sentence structures.

You may have a favorite way of expressing yourself. If you believe you may confuse the reader by using your normal style, edit your material to a more suitable style. Avoid complex words; use three short words instead of one long one if that long word will stop most readers. Once you stop a reader, you may lose him.

Punctuation is also important. Don't stop your reader by using too much punctuation or confuse him with too little punctuation.

You may be admonished in some textbooks not to "speak" to your reader, but think of him always when you write. Are you directing your material to him? Are you making your strong points strongly? Are you possibly minimizing good points only because they require but few words to describe them? Are you pacing your material? Keep the personality of the reader and his reason for reading as constant reminders of why you are writing the article.

Keep your writing simple and as grammatically correct as possible. But if you ever have to make a choice between grammatical perfection and clear communication in the vernacular, choose communication every time.

HONORABLE SPEAKER TOLD JOKE

Not long ago, an American technical expert was invited to speak before a large audience in Japan. An interpreter was present to translate the speech. The American started his talk with a lengthy story, the point of which was a humorous play on words relating to his topic. His purpose was to loosen up the audience before going into the "dry" matter of the technical presentation.

This particular joke took about five minutes to tell. All during this time the interpreter said not a word. Then, when the speaker had finished, the interpreter said a few words in Japanese, whereupon the audience broke into gales of laughter.

After the meeting the speaker, who did not understand Japanese, asked the interpreter how he had managed to capture the entire joke in so few words. The interpreter replied that there is no proper way to translate humor from one language to another, so after the speaker had finished he told the audience in Japanese: "Honorable speaker has just told a joke."

The point is that the speaker did not know his audience. Fortunately, his interpreter did.

If you are a surrogate writer, the "author" on whose work you are reporting may not know his audience. You should. And just as the Japanese interpreter did, you should protect your author from saying something the audience will not comprehend. You can do this by watching your writing style and including only those ideas and concepts in your article that will be meaningful to the reader.

KNOW THE PUBLICATION

Far too often the author tries to write for a publication he has never seen. This is foolish and is a recipe for failure. You cannot know what to do if you have never seen it done, cannot know how to approach a topic if you have not found out what kinds of subjects the editor publishes.

As noted earlier, it is important to look over copies of the journal in which you wish to publish. This helps reassure you that you are planning your article for the right reader. You can also learn a great deal about the editor's style by reading his bylined articles. Then you can write your article in a manner compatible with his style.

While the editor may accommodate your request for a copy of his publication, don't count on it. Editors are busy. You may just be adding to the work he has to do, and he has no assurance that you will ever contribute anything worthwhile. If you ask the editor for a copy, it may be two or three months before he gets around to sending it to you. If you are a free-lancer or a public relations specialist, you are probably better off getting a copy of the publication from a library, a friend in an advertising agency, or some other source.

GOOD GRAMMAR HELPS

Grammar is a tool of the writer. He can use it for effect as well as for communicating. If a writer's grammar is poor it will probably impede communication. If it is too perfect and impeccable (according to experts in such matters) it may also impede communication, especially if some ideas are best presented in the vernacular.

We all tend to speak colloquially, using grammatical forms that serve us well in our oral communications but are not technically correct. For example, an author may be told to "write like you speak." That expression is ungrammatical; a strict grammarian would alter it to read: "write as you speak." But some readers would interpret this as referring to simultaneous speaking and writing. Good grammar, poor communication. The best solution is to rephrase the statement in a way that is both clear and grammatical.

Consider using the vernacular rather than adhering to what is technically correct. Among the constructions that work at times are split infinitives, plural modifiers with singular subjects, partial sentences, and understood subjects. If a speech has been presented in an acceptable and comprehensible manner it probably will be acceptable in similar form as a written article.

If you have occasion to use translations of technical material keep in mind that the literal wording is not always fully satisfactory in translation. Words and constructions which comprise the vernacular in one language tend to be rendered as bookish in verbiage and construction in translation. As such, they fail to adequately convey full and proper meanings, and sometimes actually distort the intended ideas.

FIND YOUR OWN STYLE

Once you have started to write, select a style that suits you. It is not really important what style you prefer as long as the editor has not indicated he has any objection to it. If you choose to write in the first person, do so. If you prefer to write in the third person, do so.

If your natural writing style is a punchy one with short sentences, this is fine. It makes reading and comprehension simpler, keeps ideas flowing. If your style calls for long sentences with parenthetical material, use that as long as it is appropriate. This style will appeal to the intellect of many readers.

When a reader starts an article he falls naturally into the writing style of the author. He does not have any particular expectation of what that style will be. Just as two actors can play the same part, each proficiently and each with his own style, two authors can do likewise. Both will communicate. Both will succeed.

Most business publications do not have a consistency of style throughout as would be the case with a book to which a similar group of writers have contributed material. Each article, therefore, carries the style of the individual author. Some authors are not comfortable with a style yet try to use it because they think it will work better. It does not. Your own most natural way of communicating will work best for you.

Even if you think you are not writing in the manner that you learned as a freshman in college, have no fear. If your article is well organized and you are writing in a manner that is comfortable for you, the editor should have little trouble. He may be able to edit your material with little more than a comma here, a period there, a subhead, a reference, and so forth. He may do a little polishing—as little as he can get away with, since he has so little time—and you will be so pleased with the results that you will wonder how you wrote so well. Having given the editor a solid structure and readable style you will have given him something substantial. Both of you will be pleased with the results.

CLICKING "K"s AND SIBILANT "S"s

Try to read aloud a sentence containing like sounds that impinge upon each other and you will uncover a source of comprehension difficulty. Yes, the literate reader should read only with his eyes—but does he? In reality, he reads with both his eyes and his lips. If he sees a construction that does not sound natural in spoken language, he may halt. This is one reason why copy written for oral delivery, especially on radio and television, is so carefully edited for smoothness. Your writing should do the same.

You will find that your writing reads smoother if it speaks smoother. Flowing words promote the flow of ideas. Avoid using words that "fight" each other. Tongue twisters are stoppers.

As an exercise, try to write some material with these unpleasant combinations of words and then read them aloud. Select one word with a final letter k and a following word with an initial sound of the letter k. Do the same with the letters s, t, l, and p. You will find that there are other letters which are unsuitable as well. For instance, "black cats" will sound like "black ats" or "bla kats"—or is it "black hats"? Writing that communicates best tends to avoid these difficult elisions.

GENERAL STYLE GUIDES

There are any number of good style guides. You can't always anticipate a particular editor's preferences, but if you follow one style guide consistently, you will generally meet the standards of even the most demanding editor.

Standard style guides, available at most bookstores or from the U. S. Government Printing Office, include the *Associated Press Style Guide*, the *Style Guide of The New York Times*, the *Manual of Style* of the University of Chicago, and the style guide of the U.S. Government Printing Office. You may have another that will be just as good as these.

These guides will agree on most points. But since the *Associated Press* and *New York Times* guides have been prepared with general print media and general audience in mind you should use them with discretion; they may not work well for technical material. The Chicago *Manual of Style* is geared toward the preparation of college papers, postgraduate theses, and the like. If you are writing a technical paper—actually a short dissertation—for a business publication that carries fairly academic material, this guide may be useful. But its recommendations on some matters may be too academic for readers of business magazines. In most cases, technical material prepared for a general business publication should follow a style that appeals to the widest audience of the journal.

The style guide of the Government Printing Office is most widely applicable. In addition to material on style it contains a valuable store of information on government and diplomatic terminology.

SPECIAL STYLE GUIDES

The unique requirements of various sciences and technologies have spawned a variety of special style guides. These tend to exist in fields that have a large specialized literature and utilize many special terms (frequently quasi-Latin). The medical field, for one, has its own special style guide. Some companies have their own style guides that are used in preparing proposals, reports, and internal publications of both a technical and nontechnical nature.

In the course of writing such style guides the authors have always had to rely heavily on the standard material available in general guides. Only a small fraction, certainly never more than 10 percent, of any of these special guides pertains uniquely to the field it purports to cover. Such guides are usually designed to be complete references, obviating the need to refer to other guides. If you are writing for a publication in a field for which a style guide exists, you should be familiar with it and generally should follow its recommendations.

STYLES HAVE A FASHION

Writing styles have a fashion. At any given time some are in and others are out. The more closely you conform to the current fashion, provided it is suitable for the article, the better will be your reception by the readers.

However, a distinction should be made between fashion and fad. Avoid such fads in writing as emulation of the speaking manner of a particularly popular entertainer. Entertainers go out of the public eye very quickly. Although such a style may be suitable for some consumer publications, it is totally out of place in a business or professional journal. If, however, you are quoting someone in an article, you certainly will want to use his words in the way he uses them.

AVOID SLANG

Don't ever use slang or other faddish language. Slang tends to have a local or provincial flavor, its meaning changes over time, and it may detract from an authoritative tone. Many business and professional people are not familiar with the current teenage jargon, the cant of the television and stage industries, and the "street language" of urban communities. You will not be spicing up your story with such terms; you will be confusing your reader. You will confuse him totally if his native language is not English.

Also avoid words and usages that are acceptable in your region of the country but are not as well known or well accepted in other regions. If you are writing for a journal with an international audience stay with correct, formal language and structure, modifying it only when the vernacular is more communicative. Even readers in other English-speaking countries will not generally understand American localisms.

You can keep within the bounds of good practice without becoming pedantic. Pace your writing and keep your words simple. You should never have to resort to the use of slang. If you do, your writing and your article will suffer.

THIRD PERSON: THE MOST COMMON

If you tell a story and keep yourself out of it you have a presentation in the third person. This is the style most easily handled, although some writers of engineering and scientific articles seem to have great difficulty with it.

Editors usually prefer a third-person presentation, and it is an easy style to maintain, especially for a writer who had not been involved personally in the circumstances he is reporting on. It is the style of the daily newspaper or the TV news story: reporting on events from a distance, as an observer.

We all use it every day, with all sorts of people. Nevertheless, there will be times when you, as an author, will have trouble with it. This often happens when some portion of your narrative involves value judgments, judgments that you are professionally qualified to make but that you know may change your apparent vantage point from that of disinterested observer to active participant. Here it is generally best to go into the first person.

Sometimes you will set out to write a wholly descriptive article and find that value judgments have crept into the piece. This poses no real problem; you can take them out in the editing. Editing is always easier than writing. When you write your draft you have to keep the ideas flowing. You can modify the words later.

SECOND PERSON: GOOD FOR INSTRUCTIONAL ARTICLES

If I tell you how to do something—as, for example, how to follow instructions in a technical manual—I would be writing in the second person. This book is written primarily in the second person.

A second-person discussion can either be in imperative form ("Open the door") or in just the simple second person ("You then open the door"). The form you use depends on the context. In articles, the imperative form often is not well received because it seems dictatorial. Nevertheless, it might be the best form for certain how-to discussions.

In an instructional article you may wish to use the third-person form to explain the instructions and then give the directions themselves in the second person.

FIRST-PERSON SINGULAR

The first-person style is extremely useful in reporting on work that you have performed yourself. It is used often in magazines such as *Scientific American* and in professional journals. There is no reason not to use the pronoun "I" when the report is about your own work. Total avoidance of the word "I" can lead to stilted prose.

Nevertheless, I would make a plea for moderate use of the first-person style. If you generally stay away from the pronoun "I" you will find that it works very effectively when you do choose to use it.

To maintain balance of style you will probably want to explain your ideas in general terms as well as from your point of view. When you introduce a subjective judgment state at the outset that it is your idea and may not be subscribed to by other researchers. Your view will be respected as a considered opinion coming from a qualified source.

Use the first person when you are writing a report of your own experience. It is appropriate to describe what happened to you when telling about such events.

THE INTERVIEW FORM

The interview or question-and-answer form does not appear frequently in business and professional journals. But when it does, it is a welcome change from pedantic, didactic, how-to articles, self-serving case histories, and the like.

You don't really have to interview someone to write an article in the form of an interview. You just need to find an expert in the field who would be willing to lend his or her name to the article and review it after you have written it. You may need the help of other people in devising questions and answers.

If you propose to submit an article with the question-and-answer approach, make certain the editor really understands what you plan to do. This is a tricky style. It is often best left to the professional staff editors who work with the concept frequently. If you can work with it, by all means use it.

When starting your articles, you need a paragraph or two of introduction. All further explanations and justifications can be put into question-and-answer form. Sometimes you can build up to your climax, or conclusions, by using this give-and-take style. Keep the questions short, the answers not much longer. If either the questions or the answers consistently run over 50 to 75 words you may lose the sense of spontaneity that you are trying to obtain with this style. The interview may drag, and the reader may feel the questions and answers have been rehearsed. Interview-style articles should be fairly short. It is hard to maintain a high level of anticipation for more than a few printed pages.

Use this style carefully, but there is no need to be afraid of it.

MIXING STYLES

Should you ever mix writing styles? Of course you should—if you can handle it.

You mix styles all the time when you talk: you may tell a personal story, give someone instructions, and so forth. When writing, you just have to be more aware of when and how you mix them. Your style is your way of getting ideas across and drawing your reader closer to you. You can be personal in some places in your article, impersonal in others. For example, when you report on your own work, you will tend to be much more personal than when reporting on the work of a colleague or on the literature from which you drew inspiration. This you do almost without conscious thought.

In an article you may use one style for one part, another style for another part. By varying your style you can vary the impact of what you print. Try to use only a few styles in any single article. Too many styles may cause loss of continuity.

Some authors keep interest high by providing a change of pace just as the reader is tiring of the current tempo. When you vary the pace you must do it with skill. This usually involves changes in word length as well as sentence length. A mixed style works well and can help greatly to maintain reader interest in material that is dull but essential to your exposition.

CLEAR AND CONCISE

The story is told about newspaper columnist Earl Wilson that when he was a reporter his writing style was so distinctive that it could not be edited to conform to the style of the newspaper he worked on. This was not, despite his later successes, an advantage. On the contrary, it was such a serious drawback that the editor began assigning him to cover only certain types of stories.

As it happened, Wilson's style was fine for the type of reporting that he later developed into a prosperous career. You may not be so successful when you write a single article for publication in a business or professional journal. Distinction in writing is admired; distinctiveness often is not.

Any style that you use should be clear and concise. Some styles that are effective orally do not work well in written form. Styles of writing that find little favor among editors include short, punchy sentence fragments; long, involved sentences with convoluted phraseology; short sentences unrelieved by longer, explicatory sentences; and interminably long paragraphs. In a nutshell, moderation in style is just as important as moderation in content.

ABBREVIATIONS

You don't need to be too concerned about abbreviations but it helps you to know an acceptable style. Follow the standards that are available to you. Always spell out the full title when you first introduce a term, then give the abbreviation in parentheses.

One outstanding guide, or "standard," for abbreviations is published by the Institute of Electronic and Electrical Engineers (IEEE). It was compiled in conjunction with the Society for Technical Communication (STC) and is definitive, with metric measures included. There are standards that cover other fields as well. The American Chemical Society has one for chemical terms. The *U.S. Government Style Guide* covers place names in the United States and also gives correct abbreviations for governmental and diplomatic titles. Whatever your preference, be consistent throughout your article.

Most editors are less concerned with your article's abbreviation style than with the internal consistency of the article itself, particularly if it is bylined. If your article is consistent logically, you will not have any problems on this score.

If you use abbreviations for formulas make certain they are explained, either in a table or when they are first used. Don't assume that because the reader is skilled in the technology you are writing about he will understand all your terms. Some professional and technical journals enjoy an interdisciplinary readership. The same symbol may mean different things in different disciplines.

PUNCTUATION

Since this is a book not about writing but about marketing, no lessons will be given on how to punctuate. Just choose an accepted style guide and follow its recommendations. If you do this you will find that your punctuation will be acceptable to most readers.

Just as writing styles have fashions so do styles in punctuation. In the United States, newspapers in the East punctuate more than newspapers in the West. The University of Chicago *Manual of Style* calls for more punctuation than the style guide of the Associated Press. The *New York Times* style guide calls for something between the two. Keep in mind, however, that each of these guides is designed for a different purpose. The Chicago guide is designed for highly literate professional and academic readers who are accustomed to long sentences and are seldom nonplussed by complex constructions. The AP guide is designed for a large variety of readers, with most having a high school level of reading ability. The *New York Times* guide is designed for a newspaper reader who has completed high school and gone on to college.

While you will be writing primarily for a well-educated audience, the reading level of most readers, even those of professional journals, is not much higher than that of the AP or *New York Times* guides. Business and professional journals are news publications, regardless of how you define the term "news." Keep your punctuation simple. Punctuate as much as you need for sense, and no more. If you want to add commas for effect, don't. You may stop the reader once too often early in the article—and lose him.

REFERENCES CAN BE TROUBLESOME

If references are required they should conform to the style of the journal insofar as possible. This is not always easy because some organizations have a unique prescribed style for their reports and publications. No editor will turn down an article because the references are not in the journal's preferred style, but he will probably ask you to revise them to conform.

In most professional fields, accepted styles have been established with which everyone is familiar. The journal that publishes your article will probably use the same style as your company or organization. You may run into some major differences in reference style when you cross disciplinary lines. If, for instance, you have used the style of the electronics industry and are writing for a chemical process journal, you may not be familiar with the style used in the chemicals industry. If you use the style of the electronics industry you will most probably have no problems on this score.

If your material has to go through a review process you may be expected to conform in the most minute detail to certain formal requirements. The references will generate the most difficulty, but you will have to follow the prescribed style. Be alert to this possibility before you start to write; have the editor send you the applicable style guide. By preparing your references in the required style, you will save yourself work later on.

WATCH OUT FOR CAPITALIZATION

Use your style guide to determine how and what to capitalize. If in doubt, and if you have no specified capitalization guide to follow, use the style of your local newspaper. In particular, be sure not to use capital letters excessively. Engineers and scientists are prone to use capital letters where small letters belong, particularly with nouns. This is the style used in German, but in the English language nouns should be capitalized only when they are proper names or place names. Certain personal titles may also be capitalized. If you are quoting from another language use the proper capitalization form for that language. Incidentally, quotations should be precise and should not be paraphrased unless you so note.

GIVE THE EDITOR A BREAK

Errors in capitalization, abbreviation, and other details are often a source of major irritation to editors. Editors try to edit material carefully but may easily miss one letter in their editing. They may then catch the error in the proofreading stages, but now it costs money. Any changes made after the material has been set in type, called "author's alterations," must be paid for by the journal. The typesetter pays for errors he makes. If an error gets past the proofreading stage and is then discovered, correcting it is even more expensive. If many errors in capitalization or punctuation must be fixed, the editor will start thinking about the cost of publishing your article—not a welcome situation.

Therefore, when preparing your article for submission, watch carefully for any errors that you or your typist may have generated. Make certain that all punctuation is where it belongs, that all capitalization is correct. Editors are not being picayune in their concern about such details. Punctuation and capitalization are essential ingredients for ease of communication. Don't be cavalier about them. Show consideration for your editor in these areas. There will be enough other areas where you cannot be of help.

When you are not sure about style just be consistent in what you do. If you have followed a poor practice consistently, it can be found easily. If your style varies radically from page to page, it may be very difficult to correct, and some inconsistencies will surely slip by.

PROTECT TRADE NAMES

You must protect trade names used in your article, whether those of your company or those of other firms. The editor is not responsible for knowing what names are trademarked and copyrighted. Your legal department may make efforts in this direction, perhaps sending out all manner of letters to business press editors notifying them that the company owns certain trade names and that they should be published with a registration mark. But you also need to make an effort to protect your company's names and marks in your writing. If you do not, all the efforts of the legal department may be valueless.

There is a legal difference between a trade name and a registered trademark that the editor may not be concerned with but that you, as an author, need to know about. A trade name is any term that a company uses to identify its products. A registered trademark is a trade name that is officially registered and can be used only by the company in question. A registered trademark is designated by the symbol ®.

The editor will not usually want to have the ® symbol in the article, so he will place the name in quotation marks or spell it with initial capital letters. This suffices to establish the uniqueness of the mark and give it legal protection. Capitalizing the name indicates that the term is a special one.

You, the author, will need to protect the trade name in some other ways as well. First, in an initial reference you should use the name only as an adjective, not a noun. If you use it as a noun, it may lose its legal protection. This is how Du Pont lost "nylon." If it were still a trade name it would be designated as Nylon, with an initial capital letter.

Whenever you use the trademark, follow it immediately with a short term that describes the type of product or service. This requirement is why you will always see Du Pont's "Dacron" described as "Dacron" polyester fiber. Once the trademark and its descriptive term have appeared together it is not necessary to repeat the descriptive term in further references. The name may be used as a noun frequently, in the same manner as in conversation. It will still be protected legally. It is assumed that the mention of the trade name without the accompanying description is a form of shorthand.

Many editors are not fully conversant with the law concerning trade names but they know the name should be treated in a special way. If they know the legal way to designate a trade name, they may actually protect you from making errors. But you can't count on such knowledge. You may not be so fortunate if your material goes through the hands of a junior editor whose only exposure to business has been in the local supermarket or college bookstore.

POLISHING

No editor ever has enough staff or enough time to do the kind of editing he knows can be done, the kind he would like to see done on his magazine. If he spent all the time necessary to do final polishing he would be expending so much time and talent that he would probably be fired as a poor manager. Editing is one facet of a profit-making operation. Even when a journal is nonprofit there are limits on the editor's time.

You as a writer will be working under similar pressures. You are not likely to face the same time pressures unless you have made a commitment to complete an article by a certain date and have muffed it. The editor, on the other hand, has a deadline that is immobile, come snow, high water, postal strikes, vacations, conventions, and illness. He has to get that message out on time.

You may find that you cannot polish your material to a high level of quality because personnel in your organization have failed to meet their commitments on time. If you have promised the editor an article for a certain issue and you fail to meet the deadline, you may have lost your opportunity to get that article published. You need to watch deadlines just as he does.

If you can bring your stylistic standards to a high level and still deliver the article on time, you will satisfy the editor's professional standards—standards he cannot always meet but always strives for. A well-written, stylistically smooth article is a shining light in the average business publication. It will be treated with love and respect. The copy editor will also dwell lovingly on an article that is a model of good prose, even if the subject matter may be as enticing as sewage treatment.

Another way you can help the editor is by submitting your material in clean typed form. If you have a stylistically poor article the editor may have to retype it after he edits it. Editors of business publications do most of their own typing. If you have typing help, take advantage of it and take some work off the editor's hands. If you save him some work you might just get into print; if you make work for him you may lose out. Another retyping is not what your typist or secretary is looking forward to, but your objective is to please not the typist, but the editor.

Give your final polishing at least as much time as you feel the editor should give it. You may well find that you can develop a smoother writing style.

KEEP THE COMMERCIAL LOW KEY

Whatever type of article you are writing, keep the commercial message subdued. It suffices to mention the company or supplier name just once or twice in the article to gain its benefits. The product should be mentioned only when necessary for unambiguous identification.

Most readers become very suspicious of articles—and magazines—that constantly repeat the name of a company that has obviously had an article written for the publication. Readers will not be fooled. The reason many editors allow a company or trade name to be mentioned too often is because they are too busy to edit out all the references. They feel the material, even with its commercial connotations, is well written and is suitable subject matter for the journal.

Too much commercialism accomplishes just the opposite of what it is intended to do. It turns the reader away from the article because it looks like an advertisement, even though it appears in the editorial columns. Don't oversell. Like a salesman who talks on and on after the customer has given him the "buy sign," the article that keeps plugging a company or product overdoes the selling. Moderation works best.

11

visuals

A PICTURE IS WORTH a thousand words. This is not really a Chinese proverb; it is an editor talking. The editor knows he can show four or five pictures in the space it takes to print a thousand words—and he is always short of space.

Pictures, charts, graphs, schematics, block diagrams, cutaways, schematisms, and wiring diagrams all dress up an article and make it more interesting and attractive. Writing is as much a matter of showmanship as it is a matter of language. An editor is always seeking good visual materials.

It is easier to communicate some ideas with pictures than with words. Certainly you can show complex material and convey certain ideas more simply with good illustrations. Comparative data are more easily shown in graphs and charts. Technical data are sometimes represented properly only by visual material.

When you plan your article, plan your visual presentation as well. As was seen in Chapter 8, artwork is a basic part of your writing, not an adjunct to it. It is basic and vital.

Usually you will find your visual materials from among your data sources, just as you locate your verbal material. Sometimes you will need to create new material. You must be the judge of which approach will work best. If permission to use material is required you have to get that permission, and it should be obtained before you submit your article to the editor. He may or may not accept your selection of artwork but he will not search out other sources in order to find a better item. If, when you have outlined your article, you feel that you should generate new artwork or photography, this is all on your shoulders.

GRAPHICS IN LIEU OF TEXT

Use pictures and artwork whenever you can if the policy of the publication is to publish such material. Let the reader look at a picture. He can bring his skill to bear to draw relationships and conclusions. Sometimes when you try to use words instead of pictures, you find you are straining to make a point that a picture could have conveyed much more effectively.

Occasionally you may use your text primarily to connect illustrations, with the text amplifying on circumstances and conditions shown in the pictures. Here the visuals are carrying the main message of your article.

A photograph may lend credibility where the written word would be suspect. People tend to believe a picture more than they will believe your description of the picture. They want to "see it for themselves." A picture is direct; a written description is secondhand. All your illustrations should carry some data without which your presentation would be incomplete. If your illustrations are creative you can use them very effectively in lieu of verbiage—and develop credibility besides.

ASK THE EDITOR WHAT HE WANTS

In your negotiations with the editor, he will probably suggest what types of photographs and other graphics to use. Get as specific as possible with him, and encourage him to get specific with you.

Ask the editor what he would like. If he suggests that you write 2,000 words and use three illustrations, do that. If the article might be published in a section of the journal that carries color the editor may ask for graphs with color separations indicated. Provide them. If you can get a promise from an editor to use your material "up front," as a major article at the beginning of the journal, you will have attained a great deal. Take advantage of this by providing graphics in suitable form.

If the editor has offered you a cover be sure to conform with the requirements very closely, because this a very important part of his magazine. If you give him less than he had in mind—as, for instance, when he has asked for fish-eye photography and you give him a flat photo—you may lose your coveted cover.

The editor knows what he wants. He will have an excellent idea of how your article fits into his overall scheme. Even when you are sure that your graphics suit the content of your article there is still the question of whether or not they suit the total appearance of the magazine. An editor arranges articles with an eye toward balance. Visual material must be alternated with running rivers of type. Too much type on page after page may alienate the reader. Good graphics will increase his interest and slow him up long enough for him to read not only your article but another article that has no visuals. Good artwork can even induce the reader to look at nearby advertisements. A magazine is balanced around its artwork as well as around other factors.

Editors will tell you what photographs they want. For example, they may tell you to photograph a component of a machine rather than the entire machine, to photograph a test setup with no people in the picture, or to photograph a huge machinery installation with people in the foreground in order to give a sense of the installation's magnitude. If you have already taken such photos, well and good; you are ahead of the game. If you have not, try to do as the editor advises.

At the early stage of negotiations, the editor may appear to be simply advising you concerning graphics. He is not just advising; he is specifying. If you submit your article and have not followed his instructions, you may get a conditional acceptance: acceptance subject to fulfillment of graphic requirements that you had thought were just suggestions.

ASK THE EDITOR WHAT HE CAN DO

If you work for a commercial business firm or are on assignment for an organization or business that is paying for your writing, you will almost always be responsible for the cost of preparing your artwork. This is just as much a part of the article preparation as the actual wordsmithing. If you are doing a free-lance assignment for the magazine you should ask the editor what he wants in visuals and what work needs to be done on them to make them acceptable for publication.

If you are working on your own—for instance, you are a consultant who has no facilities for creating artwork or you need pictures but cannot be expected to hire a professional photographer—the editor may have some suggestions or may be able to provide you with professional help. You may not have facilities for separating artwork into its component colors. The editor will advise you on how to proceed if you just ask him.

Some journals do not have facilities for creating or modifying artwork. Others have large staffs and insist on having all artwork except photography done by their staff artists and illustrators to specifications established by the journal. Find out what the editor can do and what he will require you to do.

IS COLOR ACCEPTABLE?

Some magazines use a lot of color; some use none. Find out if color can be used in the printed article. You may be able to obtain or generate artwork in color, which can be very eye-catching and technically informative. Some magazines will publish color in charts and graphs but cannot afford to print color photographs. Some will print photographs in color but cannot afford separations.

Don't send color artwork unless it is called for. If you separate your artwork into color components and the journal cannot print in color your graphics may not reproduce as clearly as they would if you had prepared the material in black and white. If you send a color photo it likewise may not reproduce as well as a good black-and-white shot. The editor will tell you what he can and cannot accept. Follow his admonition. If you send in something that you consider better it may not work at all.

Editors may sometimes tell you to send color illustrations if you have them but will add that they cannot promise to print them in color. They do not always know in advance whether the article will appear in a color section of the journal or in a black-and-white section. This is determined by printing production requirements; the editor may have few options in this matter.

PHOTOGRAPHS

Good photos are invaluable. "Good" means informative, interesting, and reproducible, among other attributes.

You will probably know if the photos you plan to use are informative and interesting. You may not know if they are reproducible. A good professional photographer can tell you how reproducible they will be. When he takes them he may ask you if the magazine is printed by letterpress or by offset printing. Because of differences in the two printing processes, the photos have to be processed differently to print properly. The offset printing process tends to deposit more ink on the page than the letterpress process. The photographer will give you a repro quality, as he calls it, that is suitable for the journal's printing method: lighter if offset, darker if letterpress.

Lighting

You should know the lighting that is needed. An editor may ask for a "flat" photo, meaning that he does not want the appearance of three dimensions. A flat picture tends to wash out shadows, causing the entire subject to appear to be in the same light, with no contrast between different portions of the picture.

Industrial photographs are generally taken flat, just as they would appear in instruction manuals. There are no "highlights."

If the editor wants you to show depth the subject would have to be lighted differently. Tell your photographer what you need and let him do the work for you. Unless you are an expert photographer yourself you are not likely to know as much as the professional.

Polaroid Prints

Your photographer may take a Polaroid picture first and ask you to approve the approach he is using. He will then take the picture with a camera that is designed to give reproduction quality prints. If you have Polaroid prints you might send them to the editor for him to select the types of shots he prefers. You can save much time, money, and aggravation in this way, but do it only if the editor seems amenable.

The editor may suggest that you work directly with a Polaroid camera for some of your photos. Many Polaroid cameras are versatile, enabling you to obtain pictures that will run half a page in width without enlargement. To avoid the necessity for enlargement fill your picture completely with your subject. You would not want to leave unessential and distracting material around the sides, top, or bottom, as this material would only have to be cropped out later in order to focus the reader's attention on the central matter.

Usually you should try not to submit Polaroid prints as they tend to be unsuitable for reproduction. On the other hand some scientific work done with Polaroid equipment is exquisite, especially in color. If it is appropriate by all means send the editor the Polaroid print. Check with him and find out which method he prefers.

Focus

It may seem absurdly obvious to state that photos should be taken in focus, but too many photos, even professional ones, are blurred. Some professional photographers have no conception of how to take industrial pictures and have low regard for the quality that is needed. Take a second picture if the first one is not sharp enough.

Glossy Paper

All pictures should be printed on glossy paper as this reproduces better than a matte print. Matte prints are designed to be nonreflective. The printing processes used for journals get better results with reflective artwork.

Borders

All prints you submit should have borders around them. The borders should be at least a quarter of an inch wide all around to allow for crop marks. If your prints don't have borders the editor may have to remove some good technical material in order to indicate size to the printer. This is an unfortunate loss of material.

Captions

When you have a caption that goes with a photograph you will generally want it to be physically integral with the photograph, on the same sheet of photographic paper. This should be done when the photo is copied from the original negative; the caption should be photographically printed along with the subject matter. The editor can then cut off the caption without damaging the photo, as he would probably do if he had to remove a caption that was pasted, taped, or glued to the photograph.

Never paste the caption to the rear of the photograph unless you provide another copy of the caption. It cannot be used without being removed, and that will damage the photo. It is best to have captions in two places; on the photo, for reference, and on a separate sheet of paper, for the editor to work with. If you have captions in two places you may be doing a little extra work yourself, but you are not creating any extra work for the editor and may be assuring accuracy in your published article.

Size of Prints

Except for Polaroid prints, and possibly photos of people, all glossy photographs should be on 8 × 10 double-weight photographic paper. (In some cases 8½ × 11 will be acceptable.) This size is standard, it is large enough that the photo is unlikely to be lost or misplaced, and photos of this size can be reduced to enable greater sharpness of image. Double-thickness paper is needed so that pen or pencil marks on the back will not show through. It is also harder to fold a double-thickness sheet. Folding can cause cracks in the photo.

Retouching

Sometimes material is retouched out of a photo. An item such as a rag or a coffee cup may have to be removed. Retouching can also avoid faux pas. The article may state that there is no leakage of oil from a machine while the photograph shows a pail to catch the drippings.

Renderings

It is possible to retouch photographs to include items that never existed in the original. Such alterations, called renderings, can be used to illustrate how something not yet in existence would appear if it did exist. They can be used quite effectively to show something that would otherwise require a lengthy textual explanation. Renderings should be done carefully or they will look faked. That is worse than not showing the item at all.

Protecting Against Ink or Pencil Transfer

When you identify your photos make sure that no marks may accidentally be transferred, or offset, from the back of one print to the face of another. One way of doing this is to place each photo behind a slip sheet. You can also place photos face to face and back to back. Another way of protecting the photos is to mark their backs with a nontransferable ink or pencil.

Photo Credits

Magazines do not give photo credits to photographers unless they have a policy of doing so, they have commissioned the work themselves, or they have assembled photographic material from more than one source. If you are asked to provide a roundup article, you may obtain photographs from several sources, or the editor might obtain them for you. In such instances he will give photo credits to the companies or individuals who provided the photos, not to the actual photographers.

If you are providing photos as part of your article the photographer does not have a legal right to credit in the article or to payment from any source except you. Some photographers mark their prints with a statement that they will sue anyone who uses their photos and does not give them credit. Junior editors are sometimes intimidated by these statements and return perfectly good photographs because they believe they are not permitted to use them. Both you and the photographer lose out.

CHARTS AND GRAPHS

Charts and graphs, which are forms of line art, can range from the simplest bar and pie graphs to tri-phase chemical analyses that require color just to be comprehensible. Be sure all your artwork is of acceptable quality. The artwork standards of most journals are not rigorous, although a few are. High quality will mean a great deal to you if you reproduce the article for sales promotion or instructional purposes (see Chapter 16). When the article appears as part of your company or organization literature the artwork's appearance will be seen as your responsibility, not as that of the editor in whose journal it first appeared.

Charts and graphs should be simple, as should all the artwork for an article. It is easy to place too many data on a single piece of artwork. Technical and scientific specialists tend to put too much data on a single chart or graph.

A common rule of thumb for visual aids is to limit yourself to 15 words and one or two simple concepts. You can double this rule for printed materials. Anything more than this will increase the complexity of your visuals and will call for study on the part of your reader—and he is not normally inclined to study your material in such detail. Use two separate charts if a single chart would be too complex.

Type Size Governs

Keep charts and graphs large enough so that the editor can reduce them without loss of clarity. Type size is the critical factor to watch. Type set in all capital letters can be reduced to about six-point type and still be legible. Type set in both upper and lower cases should not be reduced below seven points and, depending on the typeface, preferably not below eight. If you start with a type size that is too small the material will become unreadable.

When you prepare artwork keep in mind that all typefaces of similar character should be the same size when the art is printed. In other words, if one label on a graph reduces to eight-point type, an equivalent label elsewhere should reduce to the same size. In the preparation stage, however, different pieces of artwork do not have to have typefaces of identical sizes. You can work one piece of art at twice its final reproduction size, another at three times. For the first you might use twelve-point type; for the second you might use eighteen-point type. When the art is reduced and printed both will look just right and make a neat appearance.

When you prepare art, size it for reduction, not enlargement. If you do not know the size that the editor prefers prepare it in a size that is not too large but which will call for a reduction when it is printed.

Line Widths

Just as type size is reduced from a working size, lines and rules in illustrations are reduced by the same percentages. In addition to establishing a consistency of type size for final appearance you should have a consistency of line width (or weights, as they are more properly called). For example, if you have an illustration that is to be reduced to 50 percent of its original size and want a final line width of two points you have to start with a line width of four points. Illustrators and artists, who will do this type of drawing, are familiar with different line weights. This is a rather technical area; let your art director or artist guide you.

A simple way to determine whether an illustration will fit easily into a magazine's format is to know the image area (printed area) of the magazine. Most standard magazines in the United States use an image area seven inches wide and ten inches high. If you have any doubts send material that, after reduction, will be no more than seven inches wide. Width is generally the governing dimension; the depths of artwork can vary. Don't compound your problems by developing artwork that is a nonstandard size. You will have enough work just writing your article.

Ask the Editor about Proportions

Your editor may specify final sizes he wants your artwork to be. If he does not, ask him—and follow whatever rules he sets down. He will want to make sure that your material can be accommodated to the journal and that neither undue emphasis nor lack of emphasis is given by any illustration in the group.

Before you submit your visuals with the article you might try reducing them to the sizes you want them to appear in printed form. You will then very easily notice if there are differences in type sizes and in line weights. You may discover other errors as well. If you then make the appropriate corrections and adjustments, you will have standardized your material and given the editor a head start in processing it for publication.

FLOW DIAGRAMS

It is easier to use a flow diagram than to describe flow, particularly when flow paths diverge and converge frequently. It is possible to show both direction and quantity, as with charts of business volume flowing across oceans. Often the diagram is self-explanatory; no reference to the details of the diagram need be made in the text. This saves a great deal of space.

OTHER ARTWORK

There is almost no limit to the types of artwork that can be used effectively in an article. Schematics and block diagrams are always in order for certain technologies. Cutaway drawings and parts diagrams are suitable for others. Schematisms (schematics that have all parts placed relative to their actual physical locations but that have schematic connections) are useful, although quite expensive to generate. Other possibilities are flow diagrams, copies of printed matter, forms, and much more. Any of these may have a place in an article. If you can provide artwork of a type not usually seen in the journal you will tend to attract more attention: showmanship at work.

Don't hesitate to be different. Just be certain that the difference makes sense in terms of your subject and approach.

Whatever type of artwork you choose, you will have to be attentive to size, size differentials, sizes of originals, color separations, and all the other factors cited above.

ANNOTATING ILLUSTRATIONS

You may encounter a situation where you cannot take a photo that would show a particular item clearly. It may be partially hidden from view. Or you may want to show a small item in relation to a large one, with the difference difficult to portray in a photo. In such a case you might want to place arrows on the photograph and make note of this in your caption.

This technique can also be used with line art. Rather than try to direct the reader to the item by a textual description use an arrow. You could employ reference numbers as is often done with blueprints. Do not hesitate to clarify your visual material and textual explanations by using numbers, letters, arrows, circles, and so forth.

When you do this on artwork it is necessary to mount it on a rigid board. Flexing may not damage the basic piece of art but it will damage the material placed on an overlay or material pasted directly to the art. Any marks you add should be of a suitable size to allow for reduction in printing.

USE STANDARD SIZES

Unless the editor specifically asks you not to, place all line art on mounting boards. This makes the package a little heavier in the mails but greatly reduces the possibility of damage in handling. You will have support for the art, protecting it against tearing, folding, and smearing. You will also have a solid back on which to write your credits and other identification, and a mounted item cannot fall accidentally from a desk, be blown by a gust of air, and get lost. You also foil the postman who may try to stuff a large envelope into a small pouch or post office box.

When you must submit visuals of different sizes try to mount them on identical-size paper or boards. Even if some of your diagrams are quite small place them all on paper of the same size. When artwork has to be mounted place it on 8 × 10 or 8½ × 11 boards. Small pieces get mislaid.

If a piece of artwork is very large it may have to be rolled up. Don't roll artwork if it has overlays or pasted materials. This will damage it. Instead, photographically reduce the art to more manageable dimensions.

TABULAR MATTER

Tables are an integral part of your text. Frequently they are the most efficient way to present complex information. They also may function to attract attention in much the same manner as artwork and therefore will be treated as visuals in this discussion.

If you have tabular matter that is to be included in the running text, leave it there if it comprises just a few lines and columns. If it is more complex, it should be set up as a full-scale table on separate paper. This is necessary because you do not know where the page breaks will occur in your article. An awkward situation will be created if a large table falls near the bottom of the page. Short material can sometimes be accommodated; longer material seldom can be.

Make sure every table you submit is referred to by number at some point in the text. Tables should be numbered in the sequence in which they are to appear. Place each table on a separate sheet of paper rather than within the running text. Whether you distribute the tables at appropriate places within the article or submit them in a separate batch is not important. Choose an approach that pleases you unless a certain approach has been specified by the editor or by the style guide he recommends.

The reason for submitting tables on separate sheets is that the typeface used for tabular material is not always the same as that used for the body of the article. Tables and the text may be set on different typesetting machines and by different individuals.

Give each table a title as well as a number. Place the title above the table. There is no need, as with illustrations, to make up a separate sheet of table titles. The table and its title always go together, whereas with artwork the captions and the actual artwork are physically separated—each undergoes a different sequence of production steps at the printer.

As with artwork, tables should be as simple as possible. Avoid using long or overly complex ones. If your data are taken from references that you cite, the interested reader can search out your sources and work directly with them. Keep your tabular matter to the minimum that you need to support your points.

Remember that an article comprises news and most readers don't want excessive detail.

FOLLOW SPECIFICATIONS

If you are given a set of specifications regarding graphics and the physical appearance of the art, follow it. Don't deviate unless you are very skilled.

If you prepare a formal paper for presentation at a meeting or convention your visuals will have to be prepared in accordance with the rules of the organization sponsoring the meeting. Many organizations have guidelines for aiding you in converting a technical oral presentation to a form acceptable for publication in their journals. As a result of having accepted an invitation to speak, you may find that you have to prepare two sets of artwork for the same visuals, two sets of tables, and different photographs and charts for the same technical presentation.

You may have to present different data for each of the two forms. Color is more rapidly comprehended than black and white. Slides cannot carry as many details as other visuals because they are designed to flit rapidly by the viewer. You will have to trade off one value for another.

Follow whatever art specifications the editor gives you. He may have just a basic style sheet or he may have an entire book of specifications. He will send it to you after you have confirmed that you are going to write the article. Take the time and effort to plan your work in accordance with his stated requirements. If you send in the completed article, art included, to your editor and the art does not conform to his requirements he may send the entire article back to you for reworking. Your article is not likely to be rejected because you have failed to follow artwork specifications but there will be a delay in having it published.

12

---

preparing
your manuscript

BY NOW, you are well along in the development of your article. You will have assembled your data, completed your early draft or drafts, perhaps obtained preliminary authorizations and approvals to use certain material, and gotten the artwork production under way. You now are going to prepare your final manuscript in a suitable physical form.

It has been assumed throughout this book that it is you who have approached the editor about having your article published. You are the seller; the editor is the buyer, so to speak. This is a buyer's market. The buyer sets the tone. Therefore, you should prepare your manuscript in accordance with the conditions of "sale" that were established when you negotiated with the editor concerning his interest in your article. There are a number of conditions that you have agreed to, even though they may not have been stated explicitly. You agreed that the article would be suitable for the editor's purposes in both content and form.

CONTENT FIRST

It is worth repeating the importance of getting your data right and doing your research task completely and well. Regardless of the physical condition in which you submit your article the editor will consider the quality of the contents before he becomes concerned about form. If something is wrong with the form and the content is acceptable you may be fortunate enough to have your article accepted. You will have failed to comply with best practice but you may be lucky. If the content is wrong you will never get an acceptance.

More than one editor is an expert. If your editor is not one he may ask other experts to review the material if it is very technical. Even if he does not do this, he still may be knowledgeable enough to judge the quality of your material and the relative value it will have to the reader. He will certainly know, when he reads your manuscript, whether there is confusion or ineptitude in your work.

Fuzzy Thinking, Fuzzy Writing

A rule followed by technical writers is to watch grammar closely because errors in grammar are often a sign of errors in concept. It is surprisingly easy to spot errors in the most complex technical and scientific work in this way even when you haven't the foggiest notion about the topic. Lack of clarity generally results from fuzziness of thought. Nobody can write clearly about something when he is hazy about it himself. If your writing is unclear the editor will have a good reason to think that your ideas are not well thought out or that you did inadequate research.

Another way the editor can tell if you have a poor grasp of your subject matter is if the explanations require too many words. Simple ideas can be expressed simply; more complex ideas can be broken down into simpler ones. If your ideas take too many words to express, in sentences that are too long and seem to be beating around the bush, expect a rejection. The editor may not know precisely what is wrong but he will know something is amiss.

Watch Out for Obsolete Data

If your data are wrong or you have referred to material that is obsolete or discredited you can expect the editor to be aware of this. He may be quite familiar with the current literature in the field. He, just as you, knows other people in the field and knows in what esteem they and their data are held. He, just as you, knows the work that others have published and where they published them. He may, because he has this knowledge, be able to help you produce a better article. The other side of the coin is that he may, because he knows what is current and valuable, choose not to guide you at all but rather to reject your manuscript outright. A review committee, if one exists, would do likewise.

Assume that the editor is at least as knowledgeable as you are. He most likely will not be but don't risk putting yourself in the position of submitting poorly prepared material to an authority who really knows the subject.

THE IMPORTANCE OF FORM

Form involves the physical way you present your article: text and illustrations both. Have the text typed in a form that the editor will find acceptable. If the manuscript is not in a physically acceptable form the editor will have a very difficult time editing it and may not feel it is worth his time to convert it to a form he can deal with.

Editors do sometimes work from atrociously prepared material. This is seldom material that comes directly from contributors. Usually it has been prepared for some other purpose and the editor is working from it at his own option. He may have found the content to his liking and, despite the form of the material, was willing to undertake the task of preparing it for his journal. Whether he would ever undertake this task with a contributed article is questionable.

PUT YOURSELF IN THE EDITOR'S CHAIR

A good way to anticipate the reception your article will get is to imagine you are the editor. According to Dale Carnegie your ideas will always get a warmer welcome if you anticipate what the other person's point of view is likely to be. This is true in all relationships. By the time you submit your article you will have invested a great deal of time and effort in the writer-editor relationship, so get the most out of it.

Put yourself in the editor's chair and consider the conditions under which he works. The editor of a publication is a manager of a business. He manages both people and product, and is also responsible for costs. His people are professionals; his product is the editorial content of his magazine. Like a production manager in a manufacturing company, he is in charge of producing the product. He has the responsibility to get as much product out the door as necessary while maintaining acceptable quality. It makes no difference to him where he gets his product from as long as it can be "shipped"—delivered to the reader. If you help him he will "pay" in kind. It is in your best interests to make his task easier. He is always under pressure.

To know how to help the editor you will need to keep in mind what he works with and how he works. He works primarily with the written word; also with artwork, data, and ideas. The closer you can come to meeting his needs in these areas the easier his job becomes. You are the surrogate editor when you contribute an article. You should think as an editor and act as an editor when you do the writing and manuscript preparation. If you provide the editor with material that is in almost exactly the final form he wants you will unquestionably get the best possible return for your efforts. A lesser effort to meet his needs will bring a lesser benefit to you.

When you submit the physical copy of your manuscript, conform as much as possible to the editor's prescribed style and to any special requests he has made. You can't always do precisely what he wants, but whenever you can the results will be of greater benefit to you.

VIGNETTES

Many articles contain ideas that do not quite fit into the main body of the text. Sometimes it is a brief story that is related to but not integral with the main idea. You may feel that the anecdote is worth telling because it gives some flavor to the article, makes it warmer and more personal. You may be fairly certain that it will make your article more credible or interesting. You may even have a suspicion that it will appeal to the editor personally.

In such a case include the item by all means. You are right in your instinct; a short item or vignette will normally appeal to the reader, may well make the article more credible, and may make the presentation a bit less weighty, less ponderous. It will also appeal to the editor, not just for these reasons but because it will enable him to vary the appearance of his pages.

A vignette does pull the reader's attention away from the article momentarily, but it also increases his interest in the subject matter of the article and is likely to induce him to keep reading. Most editors like vignettes because they appeal to the reader, create visual interest on the page, and offer a light touch when it is needed.

SIDEBARS

The term "sidebar" is primarily a newspaper term but also applies to the business and professional press. It refers to an item that is intimately related to the main text but cannot be put into the text because it will interfere with continuity. A typical sidebar would give details concerning the instruments used in a process that is described in the main article. A vignette, on the other hand, might tell an amusing tale about how a company had to improvise because the usual equipment was not available to carry out the process.

Editors are not always very precise in how they use or define such materials. Generally they refer to either a sidebar or a vignette as a "sidebar."

FOLLOW YOUR OUTLINE

By now you have established what material will go into your main text and what will go into sidebars or vignettes. You will also have selected the visuals that you plan to use. Now you are ready to prepare the article in its final form.

Follow your outline as you write. As noted earlier, you need not write precisely in the sequence in which items fall in your outline. You can assemble the pieces later provided that you maintain your continuity or feel that you can fix continuity problems when you are through. You may need to insert some connecting passages. Just make sure the finished product is smooth and does not reflect the manner in which you chose to write.

If you have done a good job of outlining and assembling your data the writing should flow rather easily. Clean up the draft as necessary. Edit according to your wont. There is no special best way: whatever works best for you is the way to work. If you wish, you can have some friend or colleague read your material, either as you are writing it or later. You may welcome some guidance and advice as you work.

INTERNAL REVIEWS

If your company or organization requires you to do so you will need to have your finished article reviewed by appropriate specialist personnel such as attorneys, engineering managers, advertising managers, marketing managers, sales managers, directors of research and development, personnel specialists, general managers, or corporate officers. Such individuals will be checking primarily for content, although advertising, personnel, and public relations managers may also be concerned with the particular wording you use. In-company reviewers will need to check both your text and your illustrations.

PREPARING YOUR MANUSCRIPT

All the foregoing work you have done on the text of your article has been preparatory. You may already have completed a draft or two. You may have had several internal reviews of your draft and may have modified your material in accordance with the reviewers' suggestions and requirements. How you have prepared your material up to now is of no concern to the editor. But he certainly will care about the final form in which you submit it to him.

Have your manuscript typed double-spaced, with about 25 lines to the page. Below are some additional guidelines.

Paper

Use white 8½ x 11 paper. Type or copy the material on one side only. The paper should be one on which the editor can write easily. Avoid erasable paper as its surface comes off too easily. It does not take pencil or ink well; the text can smear and become illegible. Although it is easier for you to type on and to correct, the very ease that you seek can obliterate your text.

The paper can be of any quality, from mimeograph paper to 100 percent rag bond. Rag bond is not as easy for the editor to work with as cheaper paper, however, and the more the rag content the worse it is. The paper you submit your manuscript on should be suitable for marking with both pencil and ballpoint pen. Ditto paper, cheap as it is, is probably the best surface to work on; it takes all sorts of marks. Other copy paper is excellent also. If you are trying to make an impression and show how highly you regard the editor, save the good paper for letters, not manuscripts. You'll show your consideration by making the editor's work on the manuscript easier.

Margins

About one-inch margins on each side are standard for most manuscripts. Smaller margins leave insufficient space for the editor to add inserts and write necessary instructions to the printer. Larger margins waste paper. A manuscript that covers too many unnecessary sheets is harder to handle than a shorter presentation.

Some publications will send you paper to type on that has margins indicated and is marked for specific areas in which to type. Usually the paper is printed with light blue horizontal lines and has printed instructions, also in blue, that are quite specific. This special paper has a purpose. Each line is a specific length, generally designed to accommodate a certain number of characters (letters and spaces) of standard pica typewriter type. Every line you type on this paper corresponds to a printed line in the published journal. By counting the number of lines of type on your manuscript the editor can get a precise idea of how long it will be in its final printed form.

If you receive such paper from your editor stick to the instructions without any deviation. Don't be creative and don't let your typist modify the instructions. They are intended to be followed closely. Don't, for instance, leave out lines at the top or bottom because you or your typist thinks it "looks better that way." The editor is telling you what he wants and he is not of a mind to accept any variations. This concept has been very carefully developed and works well.

Such paper is not used as often as it once was because of recent changes in typesetting practices. When all typesetting was done with "hot" type—set by linotype machine or by hand and cast in metal—the spacing of letters was quite predictable. Today many magazines use "cold" type, or phototypesetting. With this method, spacing is far more variable because the computer or composing machine can expand or contract the spacing photographically to fit a line length. It is hard to predict how a given line of typewriter type will come out when set in cold type.

Although the special ruled paper no longer assures the accuracy of letter and line count that it once did, it still is a very useful tool for editors who choose to use it. The typesetting variations tend to average out and the editor can come very close to predicting the final physical area that an article will cover.

Type

Use any pica typewriter type. Pica type is the standard twelve-point type on most office typewriters. The next most popular size is elite. This is smaller than pica and is used for legal documents and other closely packed material.

You can use a typewriter with proportional spacing as long as the type is pica size. But do not use one if you have been sent the special paper just described. Use a standard pica typewriter in order to provide the specific character count per inch that the editor requires. Appropriate details will be stated in the instructions you receive.

Elite type, large-type italics, and so forth are not suitable for manuscripts. If you don't have a typewritter with the type style you should use, get one. You may have a very fine article, but if it is presented in a manner that generates too much work for the editor you can run into trouble.

Breaking Words

Except when you are using the special lined paper, do not break words at the end of a line. Don't follow style guides in this regard. They often recommend breaking a word at the end of a line if it is one that unmistakably is not meant to be hyphenated (except for its location on the line). You have no shortage of paper so do not break words. Let your lines run a bit short or long (into the margin) where necessary.

Many articles published by the business press and most articles published in professional journals require the use of technical terms. These are terms which would be unknown to a typesetter or which would not be used with their usual day-to-day meanings. If such a term is hyphenated at the end of the line, the typesetter may not know if this is a term that is normally hyphenated in its technical usage or whether it has been hyphenated for convenience.

When such terms are compounded of more than one word hyphenating them at the end of a line may lead to run-ins in the typesetting. If you have to use technical terms you will certainly not want them garbled in the typesetting. For this reason it is always better to avoid even that hyphenation which seems innocuous.

Typesetters will follow precisely the copy that is given to them. If a word is hyphenated at the end of a line they may hyphenate it no matter where it falls in the final typeset copy.

The editor has to clarify end-of-line word breaks each and every time they appear. If he misses some, he pays for the corrections. He also may misunderstand your intention, thinking, for example, that you want a special term to be hyphenated when actually you do not.

Strikeovers

"If in doubt, set the mistake." This is an unvarying rule among typesetters. If a typesetter feels that there are two possible readings he will generally select the one that is the obvious error as he sets the type. He knows that the editor or author will have to pay for correcting the error.

Strikeovers are the source of most errors in typesetting. Retype portions of the manuscript rather than transmitting copy with strikeovers. The cost of cleaning up the manuscript will probably be far less than the cost of making alterations after the type has been set.

Numbers

This is a matter in which the style guide will govern. For example, the guide may instruct you to spell out numbers from one to nine and use numerals for all numbers of two digits or more.

In your manuscript, try not to break numbers or formulas at the end of a line. If you cannot fit a number or formula on a single line because it is too long separate it in accordance with best engineering writing practice. Failure to do so may result in serious errors in the typeset copy.

If you use decimals, again conform to your style guide, and be consistent. Engineering societies strongly recommend that numerals less than 1 have a zero before the decimal point. Sometimes a typewriter does not make a clean decimal point; periods come out very light. The extra zero flags the attention of the editor and the typesetter. Typesetters lose many decimal points but seldom lose zeros.

Fractions deserve special mention. When typing a totally unambiguous fraction, such as 1/18, you can type the item with a diagonal slash to indicate the fraction line. Do not do this with more complex fractions and equations. For example, if you wish a term to appear as

$$\frac{1}{x + y}$$

and type it in your manuscript as $1/x + y$, either the editor or the typesetter may misunderstand and think this designates

$$\frac{1}{x} + y$$

Type such terms with a horizontal fraction line even though this will create extra work for your typist.

Numbering Your Pages

You can put your page numbers at the top, the bottom, the right, or the left, just as long as they are all in the same place, all your pages are accounted for, and the numbers are not likely to be dropped off when the pages are machine copied. You may wish to indicate that each page in the group is one of the total number; for example, "4 of 10." When you number the pages of your manuscript, number only the typewritten text pages. Artwork is submitted as separate material unless the editor has requested otherwise. The editor will keep the text and art separate when he works with your material.

If you have to submit illustrations with review copies you will probably be told whether to distribute the illustrations in the text following their first mentions or to place them in a batch at the end of the manuscript. If you do the former, number them in sequence with the text pages. Don't number any pages, text or illustrations, with "A"s, such as "12A." Such pages can be mislaid and nobody will be the wiser. The sense of the article may not even be changed significantly insofar as the editor could tell although vital information will have been lost.

Spacing

Double-space throughout. Do not single-space quotations, as is allowed by some style guides and is done with academic material, even if your material borders on the academic. You are preparing material for a magazine, not a formal paper. Single-spacing of any portion of your text will make it difficult for the editor to perform necessary editing and provide instructions to the printer.

Triple-spacing, unless specified by the editor, is a waste of paper. It adds to the manuscript's bulk and offers no greater clarity than double-spacing.

If your typewriter is designed for it, one-and-one-half spacing can be useful. Just be sure that the space between lines is almost as large as that obtained with standard double spacing. This technique, of course, will reduce the number of manuscript pages.

Note, however, that this can be misleading to some editors. Many of them estimate the length of articles by the number of manuscript pages. Editors use a simple formula to estimate length. For example, a standard column in a journal that is 2¼ inches wide and carries ten-point type will accommodate about 35 words per inch. Thus, a printed page of three full columns, each 10 inches high, will accommodate about 1,000 words. The average manuscript page, typed double-spaced with one-inch margins, will contain about 275–300 words. Roughly speaking, 3½ typewritten pages equal one printed page.

Using this measure an editor often will reduce a manuscript to the size he wants by eliminating some of the material. If your manuscript looks too long he may scrap more material than either he or you would wish. If your manuscript looks too short he may retain all the text in the first editing but may then have to cut it when the type has been set and the true length becomes apparent. This is an expensive time to do such cutting, and you may lose some excellent material. If the editor feels that your manuscript needs to be cut extensively he may return it to you with instructions on roughly how much to cut. He is giving you the option of choosing what material can best be sacrificed. Here, however, you may be undoing work that required you to put in a great deal of time and effort early on.

One way to head off this problem is to ask the editor in advance how long he wants the article to be, either in manuscript pages or in final typeset form. If he gives you the latter figure (e.g., four full columns), you can study a page of the journal to determine the average number of words per line and lines per column. You can then translate this into the number of words to aim for in your manuscript.

Figure Captions

If your article has numbered illustrations it is very helpful to submit a separate sheet of captions. Captions are usually set in different typeface from the text. A separate sheet helps both the editor and the typesetter. If you supply only captions attached to the artwork there is a chance that these pieces of paper will be lost, damaged, or mixed up when the editor removes them in order to place them on separate sheets for typesetting. The artwork itself might also be damaged.

Number the figure captions to correspond with the numbers of your art. Do this both on your separate caption sheet and on the captions you have attached to the art.

VISUALS

Preparing Visuals for Shipment

Place on the back of each piece of art the number or letter which corresponds with the mention and reference in the text. If you have a duplicate caption attached to the back of a photo you can put the reference designation on the caption. If not, make certain to have the designation on the body of the photographic paper. Of course, if you have unmounted illustrations on vellum, avoid placing any marks on the back that would show through in the area to be reproduced. Place such designations outside the subject area on the backs of opaque materials. Use a soft pen that will not smear.

Place the same number or letter along with the caption on the separate caption sheets. This is a sure identification system. Do not, under any circumstances, put tape tabs with the photo numbers on photographs or other visuals. They cannot be removed without damaging the visuals.

Make certain that any pen or pencil marks will not transfer when you stack the items while assembling them for shipping. Ball-point ink, china marker, some felt-tip-pen inks, and some graphite leads will transfer, even when they appear to be thoroughly dry to the touch. To avoid any problems place a slip sheet between each pair of visuals.

When you ship photographs use stiffeners in your envelope to keep the material well protected. Corrugated board or gray cardboard works quite well. Other artwork should be submitted as required. Large illustrations on parchment (vellum or drawing paper) should be rolled, not folded. Fold marks will show up in the printing. Smaller illustrations may be on parchment, mounted or not mounted, but should not be rolled.

Artwork that is to be printed in more than one color should be submitted in a form requested by the editor. If there are overlays they should be carefully set in place, attached securely, and properly marked with registration marks. If the editor does not prescribe any particular method for safeguarding your art be cautious and overdo rather than underdo. The difference between a package that protects and one that does not protect is likely to be very little in cost and effort. The difference in value is tremendous.

Identifying Visuals

Some photographs are unclear as to which is top, side, or bottom. If the photo has a wide enough border mark the top border with the word "top." If the photo has no border or a very narrow one, mark it on the back. Ball-point pen will be suitable for marking on the face of the picture; use a soft pen for marking the backs of artwork.

Identify all visuals in some manner: with the name of the article, the name of your company, your name, or whatever. The editor may send the illustrations to the printer in a separate package from the manuscript. Sometimes visuals and text are processed by totally different organizations. The editor may also bunch artwork from a number of articles and send them together for processing. Editors try to identify the pieces carefully but they can make mistakes. Your annotations will help to straighten out the situation

If you have any doubts about how to submit visuals consult your editor.

Optional Visuals

While researching or writing your article you may run across or generate visual material that is suitable for publication but which is not central to your topic. These might be appropriate for background and ancillary information and may be attractive artwork to add to the presentation of the article. Send them in and let the editor decide whether or not to use them. Do not make reference to them in your text, but make certain to have suitable captions, both attached to the illustrations and on separate pages. The editor may find that one or more of these visuals carries information likely to be interesting to his readers. He can then edit your manuscript to include these visuals.

PROTECTING YOUR ORIGINALS

If the editor will allow it send him good, reproducible copies of your visuals rather than originals and charge it as a cost of the writing and art production. It takes much less effort to copy artwork and photographs before you send them than to have to recreate them because of loss or damage.

Retouched photographs can be photographically copied. Artwork with color separations can be copied in separated form on blueprint machines, maintaining the colors that you want. There are many ways to duplicate expensive art fairly inexpensively. They will prove worth the effort.

Sometimes the editor will insist that you submit original artwork in order to assure proper reproduction. You may wish to get this artwork back. It probably was quite costly and difficult to generate so you should send it only with the understanding that it will be returned to you after the editor has finished with it. State your request in your covering letter with the article and also mark each piece of artwork with a request for its return. Make this notation on the back of the mounting board, not the face of the art itself. Include your name, address, and telephone number. There is no point in requesting any special handling procedures; you won't get them.

After your article is published all the original artwork will be returned to the editor. When he sorts through it he will turn it over and see your notation. Don't expect the material to be returned immediately after the issue comes out. The editor won't get the material back from the printer until several weeks afterward, and it may take him a while to get around to reviewing what is now old material. He is involved in a new project already: the next issue.

Editors may not bother to return unmounted, unretouched photographs unless they are expensive color prints. Retouched photos, separated artwork, original graphics, and anything that is mounted will generally be returned if you so request.

KEEP RECORDS OF YOUR ART

Keeping records of your art is somewhat more difficult than keeping track of your text. Since you will have both originals and copies to keep track of you have added one measure of complexity. This involves some cross-referencing. You will need to maintain a record of the location of the originals and of reproducible copies so should the editor ask for revision you can go back to the originals to make the required changes.

All you really have to know is where your material is; you need to have only sufficient information to make unambiguous identification in order to locate material you want to work on. There is no one best method.

KEEP FIGURE AND TABLE REFERENCES IN THE TEXT

Keep all references to art and tables in the text. It is poor practice to refer to a figure or table in the caption or body of another figure or table. The reader is likely to miss the reference and may wonder where you get your information from. The editor may miss it too, in which case you might wind up with a table or figure missing in the printed version.

The editor will work directly from your text in determining where art and tables are to be placed in the final, printed article. He will put them wherever they fall most logically, subject, of course, to physical space limitations. If he misses a reference he may place materials in totally inappropriate locations.

Make your first reference to an illustration or table at the place where you want it to appear and the place where it is first discussed. Do not refer ahead to an illustration or table before you discuss it. You will only confuse the editor, and the item is likely to end up in the wrong spot. You may, of course, make reference to material that has already appeared and been discussed. This is never confusing.

SUGGEST HEADLINES

Most articles are submitted to editors with a working title and some sort of headlines. By suggesting headlines you may point up an area of major potential reader interest that the editor, in his haste and pressure, may not be aware of. He will probably welcome your suggestions. Consider your headlines as advisory only: the editor might accept them or he might not. This decision is solely up to him. As an author you may believe you have a title that will interest or titillate the reader. You could be right but the editor will still make the final judgment.

The editor's responsibilities include writing of headlines that attract reader interest. Just as he has presumably been astute enough to recognize the value of your proposed article you must grant him the equal ability to recognize whether your headlines, abstracts, and subheads are appropriate for his audience. He holds his position as editor of the journal because of his special training and skills and because his judgment has proved right most of the time. Let him select those parts of the presentation that fall within his area of expertise.

If you insist on keeping your original headlines you may be asking an editor to reject an article that he has already accepted. It is better to just give the article a working title and suggested headlines and let the editor do his work in his own way.

Sometimes an article has to be reviewed by an editorial committee as well as by the particular editor you are working with. Usually the purpose is to check technical accuracy but other considerations may also enter. Some recent government regulations concerning equal opportunity in hiring, personnel practices, and other legal matters have been carried over into the writing sphere. The review board may want to make sure the article does not imply or state anything that is in violation of the law. As a writer you may not know that you are making a statement of this sort but the reviewer who has to check for specific items may find it.

Sometimes these specialist reviewers request changes in headlines. Corporate managements have lately grown so sensitive that, in an effort to conform totally to legal requirements, they may request changes that are ludicrous or actually self-defeating. Despite the pleas from public relations departments they may insist that the changes be made if the article is to be published. Sometimes these changes are requested just to place them on record. At times you or the editor may not wish to accept such changes, particularly if they weaken the impact of the message that must attract readers to the article.

I once sent an article to a company for approval in which one headline referred to "a one-man operation." The company, conscious of the equal opportunity laws, changed the headline to "a one-person operation." I spoke with my public relations contact at the company—a woman, incidentally—who agreed that the change was gratuitous and that her company's legal department had exceeded its mandate for review. There was no adverse reaction when the article was published as originally headlined.

Incidentally, do not suggest headlines that put the name of your company or its product claims in a prominent position. This is crass commercialism and could do more harm than good if the article were to appear with such headlines. Aside from the fact that it will give the reader an unfavorable impression, it may lead him astray form the main points you are making. Instead of relating to the reader you will have related only to yourself and your organization.

Subheads

Break up your writing with subheads. As you go from one topic to another, introduce each new topic with an appropriate subhead of from two to five words. A subhead for each three to five paragraphs, depending on the length of each paragraph, gives the editor and the reader some breathing space.

Subheads serve to emphasize major points as you proceed through your explicatory material. They also introduce ideas and set a tone for the material that follows. They should, however, be completely independent of the text, and your text should be completely independent of the heads. That is, write your text as if there were no subheads and then add the heads. The editor may later, because of space problems, have to eliminate some of your heads; you don't want any important ideas to be lost.

Subheads, like headlines, are the editor's province. He may change them to suit his idea of what will appeal most to the reader. Remember that he is seeing only the textual material you have submitted. He cannot know reasons for your headings. Your reasons must be apparent from the manuscript.

You may find that the final printed article does not include all the material you submitted to the editor. The copy probably was cut because of other problems. If you provide subheads at appropriate places you will simplify the editor's task of selection and will tend to assure that he does not eliminate material he feels is important. For example, he might eliminate a complete subsection under a particular heading because he felt it was less important than other material. If you provide subheadings in your manuscript, he will have a better grasp of what you are trying to convey and how all the pieces fit together. He may still eliminate some text and subheads, but you will have given him guidance on how best to do so.

NO BROCHUREMANSHIP

It isn't how fancy your presentation is that matters; it's how competent it is. Fancy folders, loose-leaf binders, plastic inserts—all are valueless. Even worse, they make extra work for everyone. Just take your typed manuscript and your artwork, put them into a brown manila envelope (with stiffeners if you have photographs or illustrations that are not mounted on boards), add your covering letter, and drop the whole thing in the mail or deliver it to the editor. No staples. No paper clips. Just number your manuscript pages and when you get to the end mark the manuscript with "#" or, "The End." Mark the bottom of every page except the last page with "more."

If you wish you can put the title of the article, or just the key word, at the top of each page. You do not have to put your name or the name of your company on each page. The editor will only mark it for deletion later so that the typesetter will not set it in type by mistake.

COVERING LETTERS

When you send your manuscript to the editor send a covering letter with it. Letters jog memories. If, when you send in your manuscript, you fail to give the editor some reminder concerning your previous negotiations with him, he may have forgotten all about the article and may view it as an unsolicited submission. Or he may not recall how it fits into a scheme that he devised months earlier.

Don't put trust in an editor's very fallible memory. He works with many articles promised by many authors and your article is but one of them. If you send a covering letter you lift your submission out from the rest. You also won't have to "sell" your article this time; you've already done that. You only have to make the editor aware of his earlier commitment.

Editors usually have tickler files of articles and article subjects that have been promised or which they are considering. But they don't always refer to such files. If they have a lot of other material available for publication they may not be concerned that a promised article has not yet been sent in. The arrival of the article is not critical to them. If they are short of material they may go through their files and follow up on promised items. Such a review is generally undertaken only when an article has been promised for a special issue.

Even when the editor maintains a tickler file he might not have put materials pertaining to your article in the file. He may not really expect you to deliver or may just not be all that concerned about whether the article does or does not come in. In truth, there are many articles and stories in which an editor expresses interest but does not actually care much whether or not he publishes. They may be marginal as to subject matter, reader interest, or length. If such an article arrives the editor will fulfill his promise. If it does not he will write it off when he reviews his prospects. If it arrives many months late he may reconsider his initial decision to publish it in view of changed circumstances.

If you have made any major adjustments in the approach and

subject matter that you discussed with the editor in your earlier negotiations with him note this in your letter, particularly if it is something that came up in an earlier discussion. This is a good opportunity to tell the editor about some of the problems you have run into and how you handled them. It also gives you a chance to indicate your willingness to make corrections and modifications if he should ask for them.

MAKING COPIES

Most editors do not want articles submitted in duplicate, as this can become confusing. An editor will make additional copies for his own use if he wishes. However, if your article or paper has to be reviewed by a selection committee you will certainly have to submit multiple copies.

Most editors perfer to receive the original copy of a manuscript. Send the original, if it is clean, and keep a good copy in your files from which you can make other copies. You may need to send copies to department heads; to individuals in your legal, advertising, public relations, or engineering departments; or to your firm's advertising agency or public relations agency.

Ideally you would like to keep for yourself the cleanest original from which to make further copies. Generally you should resist this temptation. It can make the editor suspicious. If you have promised him an exclusive and then submit a manuscript that has been copied or duplicated he may conclude that you have violated your commitment, unless you tell him why you're giving him a copy rather than an original. Your covering letter should explain the reason for sending a copied version.

Occasionally an author will send an article to an editor on an exclusive basis and also send copies to other editors telling them that they cannot use the material but that he would like to know if they have any interest in it. This practice is considered reprehensible by most editors. If you do this you may be destroying the very objective that the editor you are working with wants to achieve. He wants not only to have an exclusive article but also to hold onto new ideas and concepts for timely disclosure—the timing being his. If you have ever considered using this practice, dismiss the idea. You may end up having your article published in the wrong journal and you will have destroyed your rapport with the editor of the journal you prefer.

All this may have made the copy machine sound more like a curse than a blessing. But it can be a boon to the writer. One very good reason to send a copy instead of the original is to assure a neat appearance. You can strip in corrections or white out words on the original, and the submission copy will still look good. This saves the work of retyping entire pages.

When you send artwork don't send copies unless they are as good as the originals. As noted earlier, you can make reproducible copies of your artwork that are just as good to work with as the originals—and not as fragile.

Sometimes an editor will ask you to send, with your submission, good quality copies of the original art. He does not want to be responsible for using or holding—and possibly damaging—a costly original. He is aware of the cost of generating artwork and is probably doing this to save money, both for himself and for you. If his publishing company is like most, it operates on a minimum budget—and you may be working for a giant industrial corporation with more than adequate funds to repair such damage as might occur. He does not want to be responsible for this material since it is out of his control so many times during the course of publication.

If your manuscript has to be checked by a review committee or editorial board you may be asked to submit several copies of your article, art included. This is a common procedure when the journal is published by a professional society. Although the review committee may comprise as many as a dozen members, no article is ever reviewed by the entire committee. Three reviewers are considered an adequate number, each a specialist in your particular technology or specialty. In this case you would need to submit four copies: one for each of the reviewers and one for the editor. If the committee is much larger than this, the publication's editors will have additional copies made or will advise you as to how many are needed.

For the most part, carbon copies are not as suitable as machine copies for committee reviews. They are not clean enough to work with and are often difficult to annotate.

Illustrative material sent to a review committee should only be copies. Originals should never be sent to reviewers because they may make marks on them, ruining them for reproduction.

RETURNS FOR CORRECTIONS AND APPROVALS

Do expect to have to rework some portions of your material, if only slightly. You may not actually have to rework anything but be prepared. You would have to be an oracle or a magician to be able to read the editor's mind concerning what he anticipated when you first discussed your article. He knows that the result will not exactly correspond with his original expectations. Your article may be better than he expected and he may like it immensely. It may be worse and he may have doubts about the whole thing. However the article turns out, it will almost certainly be different from what he anticipated. Listen to what he has to say about possible changes.

Just as the editor trusts your professional judgment and would not presume to give you specific, detailed directions for your writing, you should not try to usurp his editorial function by being stubborn about making necessary adjustments to your material. Let the editor decide what he wants to do. Accept your own human fallibility. You have tried your very best and this is what you have come up with but don't insist that it is perfect. Be flexible. The editor will generally give you the benefit of the doubt unless you have strayed much too far from the original concept or your manuscript is poorly executed.

If a review panel asks for some modifications of your text this may involve researching some data you were not aware of. The editor will send you the manuscript and generally a copy of the findings of the committee or a description of the decisions they have reached. You would then make the necessary corrections and changes, assuming that you are amenable to them, and would return the material to the editor. He may or may not resubmit the material to one or more of the reviewers to verify. Whether or not this is done depends on the complexity of the rework and the rules of the journal or society.

A detailed description of how to proceed to get approvals is given in the next chapter.

Besides possibly asking you to make corrections the editor may send your material back and request that you get approvals. Approvals are actually much more important than corrections. Your manuscript has presumably been submitted after a thorough review of its contents so the text is basically correct. But are you "cleared" by all parties?

You might already have had to obtain some approvals in order to obtain data. You now may have to get approvals for the finished article. The editor will certainly not want to obtain such approvals himself unless he told you earlier that he would do so. You must assure him that you have obtained all clearances to publish.

If you have the approvals the editor will not usually ask to see them. This is your responsibility. You must be especially careful if your name or the name of your organization is given as part of the byline of the article. If there is any onus it will not be on the editor because he will have accepted your word in good faith.

13

---

getting approvals

RECENTLY I received a manuscript of an article from a major industrial company that advertised regularly in our publication. It concerned one of the firm's products and was about a customer that subscribed to our magazine. It was well written, well prepared, and it was a good story. It fitted into the editorial style of the magazine and would need almost no editing. In short, it was a good industrial article. It should have been a perfect fit. But it wasn't.

There was one problem that became apparent the moment I read the article. The customer about which this story was written had obviously *not* approved its release. How could it have? The company name was misspelled—not once but several times. This never could have happened if the company had submitted the article to the customer; there is no one who doesn't know how to spell his own name.

Knowing the public relations people at the customer company, I promptly called up and asked if they had approved the story. This was a fairly ridiculous question because I could tell that they had never seen the article.

Their reaction was one of shock and thankfulness that I had called them. No, they had not seen the story. No, they would not approve it as I described it over the phone. They asked me not to publish it and asked me to send them a copy immediately.

Four days later a letter came from the company that had submitted the article asking that it not be published. No explanation was given but the customer, the writer's company, and I all knew why: someone had goofed, and goofed badly.

This type of *faux pas* was unusual for the astute public relations department of the industrial giant that submitted the article. Normally they would never let such a story go through without a routine sign-off. But it slipped by them.

This story is not unusual. The moral of the story is the importance of making sure all necessary approvals are obtained before sending a story to an editor.

GET APPROVAL TO WRITE THE STORY OR ARTICLE

Even before you start to plan or write an article get approvals from any people and companies that will be named in the article. Make certain that they will allow you to publish an article on the topic you have in mind. They might let you write for internal publicity but not for general publication. It is best to find out before you do much work. Do this before you even plan the article. If a customer of your company, for instance, will not let you talk about what you have done for him then forget about that article. It simply will never get approved.

When you need to obtain data directly from someone at the company you plan to write about you may need permission to enter its plant or facility. This can sometimes be quite difficult especially if the proposed story serves no sales or public relations purpose for the company. Sometimes a firm may feel the article would be detrimental to it, although it would benefit your own company or the client for which you are writing.

This, of course, poses a very difficult problem: how are you going to write the article if you can't get to the original sources? The company may refuse you the opportunity to speak to the people who are best informed and to view the equipment or facilities about which you plan to write. It may even refuse you permission to publish the article at all if you so much as mention the name of the company or identify it in any easily recognizable way.

If you run into this sort of situation your only recourse is to recast your ideas in a different form, one that does not rely on first-hand information from the company. You will have to try to find a suitable secondary source, as was discussed in Chapter 7.

GET APPROVALS FROM ALL SOURCES

More than one company or individual may be the subject of your article or be mentioned in it. You must get approval from each one. Any one disapproval may kill your proposal to write. Any disapproval after you have completed the article will prevent its publication. You are solely responsible for getting all approvals unless the editor specifically, and in writing, has agreed to get approvals for you. Otherwise, expect your editor to question whether you have received approvals from all sources. Keep in mind that an approval received from the proper department may be all you need from one company while you may need numerous approvals from numerous departments when dealing with other companies. You need "yes"es from all reviewers. A single "no" kills the article. You may not necessarily have damaged your chances for publication of the article even if you have missed one major reviewer. A late approval can be obtained as long as the reviewer has not previously given you a negative response.

The position and standing of your editor may enable him to get some material approved that you could not. He can often, through personal contacts and the prestige of his journal, obtain permission for your article to appear. He can go into a plant that you would not be permitted to enter. The people he deals with have dealt with him before: they know him and presumably know his reputation for honesty and probity. They trust that he will not disclose anything he sees to a competitor.

You, on the other hand, may be writing for a company that does business with the customer you want to discuss in your article. That customer may know that a sales or trained representative employed by your company also goes into plants of other companies: competitors. Regardless of your firm's reputation and your own reputation as, perhaps, an extremely cautious and proper individual, the customer has no assurance that you will be chary about sharing the knowledge you gain from seeing a specific installation. If you are a sales representative yourself, it is even more unlikely that you will be allowed into a plant for a story, since salespeople do not enjoy an overall good reputation for being closemouthed.

Besides approval to enter a plant you may need an approval from the manufacturer of an item if you use an illustration of one of its products, a general approval from corporate management, or approval from managers in the firm's marketing, engineering, advertising, legal, or other departments. Some companies insist that every article be "signed off" by every corporate department whose specialty is involved in the article. Watch all the procedures and follow them. To miss even a single one may spell death to your article.

This is not to say it is difficult to get such approvals. Approvals are surprisingly easy to obtain. They are simply pro forma in many cases. If the company for which you work has a public relations department the people in that department will help steer your material through the maze. They are professionals who know how to get around the obstacles.

When you submit your material for review include the entire manuscript. This means everything that is likely to be published with your article: all text, all footnotes, all references (although not the books or articles that are referenced), all artwork, all photographs, everything you plan to send to the editor and want to have published. Withhold nothing when you want your approvals. You may find that the one item you left out was the most sensitive one and that you now have to eliminate the item or modify the article, perhaps at the cost of considerable time and expense.

DON'T TRY TO INFLUENCE THE REVIEWERS

Whatever type of approval you are seeking to get—by specialists within your company, from the editorial board of the journal, or from the company you are writing about—written sign-offs are required. If you know some of the reviewers you may be tempted to try to obtain favorable review of your material. Squelch this temptation. If you do not know a reviewer and you feel he might react unfavorably you cannot influence him. Any contact you make with him may be construed as interference and as an attempt to get favored treatment. If he is an antagonist already you will only antagonize him more.

If the reviewer is a friend make sure he continues to be a friend by not placing pressure on him. He probably will give you all the benefit of doubt. He may even confer with you during his review. This is his option, not yours.

When you are dealing with a committee of experts your editor is the go-between between you and members of the committee. He is your surrogate and advocate and will always try to work in your behalf because he has already indicated his desire to see your work published. With such a technical review, unless your entire concept is rejected you will have an opportunity to change your material if the reviewers think this is desirable. You may not like the direction you are being told to take but you can settle differences of opinion after the review has been completed. Don't ask for trouble by anticipating problems that may never arise.

Some journals have a policy of publishing only articles that have been submitted first to a committee for review and selection. Here, the foregoing admonitions about dealings with reviewers are even more important.

THE REVIEW PROCESS

Each person who has to sign off the article will check his particular specialty with extra care. He may make changes that he feels are mandated or may just make suggestions for changes. If the changes are mandated you have no choice but to make them if you want your article published. Often the sign-off is given only conditionally, subject to the specified changes being made.

If you strongly disagree with a mandated change obtain professional public relations assistance if any is available to you. Or go to your editor with the problem. Many of the people who will have to sign off on your article are experienced with this type of thing. They know that the editor can overrule them—and will—if he desires. You, and they, are in the clear if something untoward should happen. The most likely untoward occurrence is a questioning note from a high-level executive inquiring about why something he noted was or was not published in the article. If you and the reviewer can show that the latter requested the changes but the editor did not accept them, the executive will generally accept this as explanation enough. If the reviewer never requested any changes, the executive will also probably accept this explanation, presuming that the person who signed off on the material had the authority to do so. Top executives do not generally second-guess their managers.

If the company you are writing about is an advertiser in the journal the editor is more likely to comply with requests for modification. If there is no likelihood that the company will ever advertise he will probably opt for the story that makes the most interesting reading.

Sometimes when you have to obtain approvals from the company you are writing about a representative of the company may insist that you make certain prescribed changes that you know will cause the article to depart from your editor's requirements. You are in a dilemma. Confer with the editor and explain your predicament to him. In this type of situation trust the editor's judgment. If he wants the story badly enough and thinks the prescribed changes will damage it he may speak to the company representative and get the approval. He will usually get what you wanted although wording may have to be changed to cover the disputed point. Sometimes the editor will know the recalcitrant signatory personally and can reassure him that all intentions are honorable. If you run into this type of situation don't try to handle it alone. You will always lose. Let the editor work things out for you.

QUOTATIONS MAY HAVE TO BE CHANGED

You may have quoted someone quite accurately as saying that "something stinks." He probably won't want that specific wording to go into the article. He would rather it be stated more euphemistically; for example, "it was not quite right." It still may stink but you can't use this picturesque type of language.

He may even deny that he said what he did. Don't try to convince him that your tape recording is accurate. It still will not get you the approval you want. You must mollify him and change his wording.

In particular, you may often find that you quote the president of a company and see the legal department turn it into incomprehensible legalese. The president is unlikely to turn to his legal counsel and tell him that the wording should stay as it was. If the purpose of having the attorneys review the text is to assure that all statements are acceptable, the president must support his advisers.

You have the problem of trying to communicate with a reader who is not an attorney and for whom the legal niceties have no meaning. You will have to appeal to the president to revise the language to some compromise between what he actually said and something that the legal counsel will accept. You may have to go through an approval process two or three additional times until you get wordings that are acceptable to all parties.

You will always have more trouble with words than with facts.

Only Good Grammar Gets into Print

How many times have you seen someone read an article and heard him mutter, "He never said that," meaning that a quote did not contain the language originally used. Such was the reaction of the American public during the Watergate proceedings when each of the participants deleted expletives. Some of them would prefer you to think they never used expletives.

Not only will expletives get deleted but grammatical structure will be changed. Expect anyone you have quoted to ask that his quotations be changed to be grammatically correct. Neither he nor you nor I speak with impeccable form—and the reader knows that. But quotations should be grammatically sound when they appear in print. The written form has certain conventions and proper use of grammar in quotations is one of them.

If you anticipate that the person you are quoting will be sensitive about his grammar change the quotation even before you submit your material to him. He will be flattered and pleased. You should proceed with your writing as if he had used the proper grammatical forms throughout. Nobody minds being thought of as educated and intelligent; everyone resents being presented as an ignorant buffoon. You may not think that the words you quoted are so bad but the other fellow does.

MAINTAIN RECORDS OF SIGN-OFFS

An editor may ask that you send him a copy of the approval signatures. This is a very rare practice, but do be prepared for it if the material you write about is controversial. More likely, your own company or organization will want to maintain records of approvals against the time when someone may take exception to something published in the article.

Your records should be maintained with care. Your records of signatories may be on a routing sheet with all details concerning the article, including dates and names of signatories. Names should be legible. If initials are used, the names should also appear. You may want to rubber-stamp the title page of the manuscript with a grid that calls for initials of reviewers and dates of reviews. Use whatever method works.

Keep such records along with signed copies and copies that

have notations for changes that you have been asked to incorporate into the final version of the article (the version you will have sent to the editor).

AN EDITOR MAY BE A GOOD FRIEND

Your editor may turn out to be a very good friend to you if you cannot get approvals within a reasonable time or if you have a recalcitrant reviewer. Here's an example of just how helpful a good editor can be.

A company that advertised in a journal could not get its customer to give permission to submit an article to the journal. The story was written but the customer continued to hold it. After two months the editor stepped in to help.

The editor asked the author to send him the article as submitted to the customer. He promised not to print it in that form but to submit a rewritten version to the author. (Incidentally, the editor did not promise that the rewritten version would be subject to another approval processing; he only promised to show the author the revised version.)

The editor scrapped virtually the entire article. He rewrote it and left out mention of the customer altogether, except to note that the product was in use. It then reflected the original conversation between the author and the editor, and included much material not originally covered by the author. It was a smashing success for the author and his company.

Several months later, at a national meeting, the author was asked by someone in the audience what company had been referred to in the article. (Reference was made to the fact that the journal had an impeccable reputation for accuracy.) A representative of that company happened to be in the audience; he voluntarily rose and acknowledged that the installation was his.

Without the cooperation of the editor the story would never have been published. The editor knew how to get around the approval process and yet have an article suitable for his journal.

IF THE MATERIAL IS TECHNICAL, GET APPROVALS ON TYPESET COPY

Some technical journals have an established policy of asking authors to reverify material after it has been set in type. This is to assure accuracy of mathematical expressions and other technical data in which symbols are needed. Too many errors can creep into typeset material when the typesetters are not familiar with the specific symbology used in the article. To attempt to publish such material would be futile because it is not possible to know whether the typeset copy is correct.

If you are the author the editor will probably send you the typeset copy to check. If you are listed as the author but are actually working from material supplied by others it would be advisable to ask each of the contributors to recheck his material. Proceed with other approvals and get signatures just as you have done at the manuscript stage.

When working with material that is set in type remember that you will need to maintain the production schedule. Your editor will probably advise you on specific due dates. Don't take too much time to complete your final review. If you do, you may miss the publication date and your article may not appear in the specific issue you had wanted.

If there are corrections to be made mark them clearly so the editor won't have to go back to you for clarification.

Take advantage of the opportunity to review the typeset copy by doing some proofreading as well. Do not read only the technical material and assume that the nontechnical text will be accurate. Errors that creep into the verbiage may turn out to be just as misleading to readers as errors that show up in formulas, diagrams, and elsewhere.

14

---

non-article submissions

ARTICLES COMPRISE the major reading matter in every business or professional publication. But they are not the only material. Most business publications and some professional journals also carry other information, such as new product offerings, new services, new literature, news about people in the industry or profession, book reviews, abstracts, calendars of events, expansion, reorganization, and other changes in companies, general news concerning the industry, legal developments, financial reports, and so on, and so on, and so on. The list is unlimited.

If you are a professional public relations consultant, you should be familiar with these by this time. If not, you should be able to find out what you don't know.

If you are asked to send out press releases for a club, an organization, an association, a school, a client, or even a friend, you should know what is expected. Be aware that there are more effective ways to get material to an editor and there are less effective ways. The purpose of this chapter is to provide some of the guidelines that will help make these types of editorial submissions as effective as possible.

Compose your release as if it were a newspaper story. Put

everything into your lead paragraph. Elucidate later, going from more important to less important material as you go down the page. When you reach the bottom of the page, stop. Adhere strictly to a one-page limit. If you feel that you have left important points out go back and prune to make room for them.

Be advised that if you put a commercial message in the first paragraph you may never see that news release in print. If the editor does not have time to read the second paragraph he may simply conclude that you have sent him a copy of a sales letter that was sent to customers. He won't publish one of those.

ESSENTIAL INFORMATION

What must be included in the release that is not part of the subject matter of the press release? (We will discuss content shortly.) Think of yourself as an editor. You want to know:

1. Who is sending the release.
2. What the subject of the release is. (Is it a new product, literature, or what?)
3. If the news can be published immediately, or if it must wait until a certain date before it can be disclosed.
4. Who can be contacted for more information, and what his telephone number is.
5. An address to which inquiries can be sent.
6. Whether special graphics can be made available, such as color photographs.
7. Who the product is to be used by, the literature to be read by, the action to be taken by.
8. What the business of the company sending the release is.
9. Anything else that is appropriate to the subject of the release.

Provide Information about the Sender

Releases are sent to editors without company names. Incredible? It happens every day. For most editors, the company or person sending the release is sometimes a very important factor in establishing the value of the release to the reader. If the sender is a major company or organization or association in the industry or profession, the editor should know that immediately. Tell him.

It sometimes helps to note on the release whether you are interested in having the release appear in the new product section, the literature section, the calendar, or some other special section or department. Give the editor a break. If you help him he will help you. If he has to guess at what you intended, he will sometimes guess wrong. You will be unhappy; he will have an unread item. To avoid that, just note the appropriate section on the release.

Provide a Release Date

Give a release date unless there is no importance attached to that date. Some news items are announced in conjunction with other events, and a premature disclosure may destroy the spontaneity and impact of the event. If you have restrictions on disclosure date, tell the editor.

Try, if possible, to have a dated release reach an editor's desk no sooner than the length of time before the publication date that is at least equal to the frequency of publication of the journal. (That is, a release to a monthly should arrive no later than one month before issue date. A release to a weekly should arrive at least a week early.)

If you want an announcement to appear in a March issue, send the release so it will arrive at the time the editor is preparing March releases for publication. This is not likely to be February or March, nor is it likely to be November. Some editors use a 31-day tickler; they hold material only 31 days. If, when the material is being prepared for an issue, you are still a month too early, your release gets discarded. That tickler file must be cleaned out. (If you are lucky the editor may have his file set up by months, not days of the month.)

Provide the Name of Someone to Contact

Give the name of an individual who editors can contact for more information. That person should be able to answer all questions and later handle inquiries that develop after publication or be able to forward the inquiries to whomever will actually handle them. One name is all you need; two are too many and will only confuse matters. If the release comes from a public relations agency and the agency insists upon its name and address on the release stationary give only the name of the company (client) contact. If the agency person can answer questions, handle inquiries, and do all the rest of the response work, then including that person's name is sufficient. But just one name please.

Would you believe that some press releases have no telephone numbers for someone an editor can contact? If you're skeptical just sit at an editor's desk for a month. You'll see releases with no telephone numbers, no name, no company, no address, no contact, and not even a return address on the envelope. You can get away with leaving out everything else (although you shouldn't) but you must include a telephone number. If a phone number is supplied all else can be obtained. An editor will not spend time asking Information. If your release is not important enough to you to put a phone number on it, it is not important enough to the editor to publish it.

Indicate where readers may address inquiries. This may be different from the address from which the release emanates. In large companies inquiries are sometimes addressed to the marketing department; the release comes from the public relations department or agency. A person's name is needed in case the editor wants to make contact for any variety of reasons, including the possibility that he may have spotted a lead for a major article. This happens more often than you might believe. An editor who knows his industry well can recognize a release that carries information about a unique or revolutionary development—a claim that the sender may be too modest to make.

Are Photos Available?

Some journals publish color photographs. If a color photo is available for a new product, let the editor know. Because color prints are expensive to reproduce, it is not necessary to send them (or transparencies) with the release. Editors must adhere to budgets, and they wince when color shots are sent indiscriminately. If you have special charts or graphs or color-separated artwork that could be used let the editor know. Put a brief note at the bottom of the page, well-separated from the text of the release. Then he can decide whether they merit inclusion.

Tell the Business of the Company

Somewhere on the page with the text of the release include a one- or two-line statement about the business of the company. This may sound like a strange request, but if you are promoting a new product that has been developed for sale beyond your company's traditional markets the editors to whom you are sending the release may have no knowledge of your company.

If your release is going only to a half dozen journals that you know well this should be unnecessary. However, even here it is not out of place to identify the company. A junior editor may handle the release and this will help him (or her) considerably.

A RELEASE IS NEWS

A press release is an announcement of news. Treat it as such. Give the news first.

A press release is *not* an advertisement. If you treat it as an advertisement it will not be printed because no payment is included with it; advertising must be paid for.

Press releases are not printed as free advertising. You will get your releases published once, twice, maybe more often. Eventually you will run out of welcome. If you are an advertiser you will always be welcome. Editorial space in a journal is not without its printing and production costs. Companies that do not advertise in a journal should realize that since the industry cannot depend upon them for support of the industry journal, their material can be discarded with little loss to readers. Editors have their blacklists; publishers compile them.

Bribes Don't Work

A type of bribery is sometimes used in an attempt to get releases published. For example, an agency will state that it wants to see how much interest a client's release creates in order to determine whether to advertise in a journal. This is so much malarkey. While companies do run advertisments and then determine the value of the ads by the number of inquiries they draw, making a determination on the basis of a press release is a shoddy practice. Advertising is an offer to sell; a news release is information. The two are not the same and readers respect that difference.

Legitimate news is always welcome. No form of flattery, bribery, or cajolery is necessary to get an editor to publish legitimate items. If you embellish a legitimate item you make it suspect and risk having the editor discard it.

REFERENCE ALL RELEASES

It seems that the art of cross-referencing is almost unknown to some PR people. They send out releases without dates or reference numbers that would identify a particular release for their own purposes. Those are the people who call frantically to ask the editor to kill the release that they sent.

"When was it sent?" They don't remember, but it was about three weeks ago.

"What was the release reference?" It had none.

"What was the subject?" It was about a new appointment and the man quit.

"Which new appointment?" (In such cases, the editor invariably works for a monthly magazine and has received four such announcements from the same company in the three intervening weeks.) The name was John Doe.

The editor's problem is that the material has long been put into the hopper for processing, and it would be impossible to locate even if the editor would try (which he won't).

Or consider this case:

A release has been sent out in error—a clerk put the wrong material in the envelope. (It was not dated.) Now how can the PR people get the editor to hold up on publishing the material? They can't. It's too late. They'll just have to forget the whole thing and try to work out the problems that come after publication.

In this case the error occurred because there was no reference number on the release, so the clerk did not have clear instructions.

Many problems can be avoided if reference numbers and coded dating information are applied for internal use. Reference numbers and coded dating also help the editor if he wants more information. He might be able to open the door to a big marketing opportunity for you if he had more information. Poor referencing closes that door quickly.

NO COVERING LETTERS PLEASE

Many company executives feel that they have to send covering letters with their releases. This is generally intended as a courtesy to the editor, but it is not necessary. Such letters are usually superfluous and are often discarded. Unfortunately, sometimes the covering letter contains information that should be in the release, such as instructions regarding inquiries, and so on.

A covering letter sent by an agency is usually an attempt to persuade the editor to publish a release that may have little or no value because the agency has received pressure from its client. It doesn't help get the release published, but it enhances the agency-client relationship.

A release either stands on its own or it doesn't. If it does, no covering letter can really hurt. If it does not, no covering letter can help.

PRODUCT RELEASE—WHAT SHOULD IT SAY?

Take a look at an example of the right way to prepare and submit a product release.

The following is the lead paragraph (names changed, of course) of a release received by an editor of a journal in the packaging industry. It obviously refers to an item which has broad industrial applications:

> A new switch-programmable limit controller has been developed by LTZ, Inc., Cocamamie, Md. About the size of a telephone and costing less than $1,000, the new Z-123 can control and time precise electrical and mechanical events on process lines or machines with extreme simplicity.

From here it goes into more and more precise detail, until, on the second page, it gives detailed engineering specifications. A note on the release stationery states: "This release has been intentionally written so that the first half will be readily understandable to the management or production level person. The second half contains technical detail that the engineer will want."

That note is actually superfluous. It describes the proper way to prepare a release: by proceeding from the general to the particular.

That release carried the name of the public relations agency. It was on a standard agency letterhead with full address and telephone number. Yet, it also included the following:

FOR IMMEDIATE RELEASE

Contact: John Smith, IV
            (121) 123-4567
Enclosure: Photo of Z-123 limit controller

The bottom of the second page (this was written on two pages quite deliberately) gave the name of the company (the client) from which the product is available. The complete corporate name and full street address, including the Zip code and telephone number, were supplied.

This release did not employ the finest grammar possible, and, in fact, stated one attribute of the product in an ambiguous manner. But it sure did communicate. The paragraphs were short, with one idea per paragraph. A notation of "-more-" appeared at the bottom of the first page so the editor would know there was more than one page. Even the picture was good: it had identification printed clearly on the front of the photo, and it had a white border. No mistakes here.

However, one item was missing—a reference number. But the product designation could be used as the release reference number, making a second one superfluous. The release did not have a coded date, but needed none. It had a headline that merely identified the product. It could have had more, but it is really not the responsibility of the release writer to interpret the value of his material; the editor should do that.

This sample is as close to perfect as you are likely to see.

Another release starts out a bit more commercially but does much the same as the preceeding release:

Measuring length or speed of web equipment or roll stock . . . metal, fabric, paper, etc.? The completely solid state Model ASL length sensors from Green Dragon Controls offer accuracy, reliability and long life even when used on high speed applications.

This release clearly describes what the product is useful for. The editor has only to know if the application is suited to his industry. He would then know the value to his readers. The style of this release is not acceptable because it interprets the value of the product; it does not state facts only. Terms such as "accuracy," "reliability," and "long life" are qualitative and should not be used in press releases. How accurate? How reliable? How long is the life? The term "solid state" is quantitative and is perfectly acceptable here because no interpretation is needed.

This release has a reference number and a release date. It proceeds from the more important to the less important. It concludes with a name and address for inquiries. It gives the full name and address of the client although it does not give a phone number. (The agency may want to deal directly with editors instead of having the client do so. We cannot presume upon motives, but the remainder of the material is too professional for this omission to have been accidental.)

AVOID VALUE JUDGMENTS

It is not the function of the release writer to make value judgments (although they do it all the time) nor is it the function of the editor to publish value judgments, either his or the release writer's. It is up to the reader to make value judgments.

Releases that purport to provide data but give conceptual information instead are not as welcome as those that provide hard facts. How accurate is accurate? How fast is fast? How large is large? If accurate is stated in terms of error rate, it might be 10 times better than any other similar product on the market. Or it might be only as good. Is fast 200 revolutions per minute or 200,000? Quantitative data are necessary so products can be compared and claims evaluated.

A junior editor bringing a rewritten release to his senior editor might be asked, "How do you know the product is fast? Do you have the technical knowledge to evaluate the manufacturer's claim? Have you seen it work?" If the junior editor responds, "It says here in the release," he should be ready to hear his senior editor say "So what? Have you seen it actually perform? If you did would you know what to look for?" The reader will be as skeptical as the senior editor but the reader knows what the answer should be while the editor may not.

You Can Never Be Sure

Several years ago a junior editor I worked with learned first-hand about not believing releases. He was working on a story for three months concerning a new sophisticated quality assurance instrument. He had just sent the approved article to the printer to be typeset when he picked up a press release that had just come in. It claimed to have developed the "first and only" such quality assurance instrument.

Surely, the writer of the release and the manufacturer did not know of the other development, which my colleague had become so familiar with. If they did, they probably would not have claimed to have the "only" one; rather they would have said "best." Their claim was brazen at worst, ignorant at best.

Editors who value the reputations of their journals will add words to the releases that qualify unsupported claims. They will atrribute such claims to the manufacturer and will never put the prestige of their publication behind such claims. Such qualifying statements include: "The maker claims," "said to be," "stated as capable of," and others. When you write releases use these qualifying statements and save the editor some work. Material that requires minimum editing obtains maximum speed of publication.

LITERATURE RELEASES

If you plan to send a literature release, that is, a press release announcing the availability of technical or other literature, plan to send a copy of the literature along with the release. You may not realize it but there are many possible interpretations of the significance of the contents. When you write the press release you may reflect the opinions expressed by the authors of the literature (individuals, company, and so on). The points you mention will not necessarily be of interest to all readers of all the journals you're interested in having the release appear in.

You may, in fact, be obscuring those aspects of the literature which are of greatest importance. This is certainly the case when the literature is comprehensive, as a brochure or full-line product catalog. You are best advised to describe the contents in terms of the data it carries, not in terms of description of the product or service or whatever is the subject of the literature. Let the editor judge the value of the literature for his readers; you will probably get more mileage that way.

More than one new brochure has provided an editor with the substance for a major article. If you include just the news of the availability of the brochure you will certainly lose some follow-up capabilities.

Some magazines use photographs of the front page of a brochure or booklet. They may even show the front page of a one-page data sheet or the title page of a catalog. Some writers like to send copies of photos. That's your option. It is not likely, however, that you will see a picture of the literature as frequently as you will see a picture of a product.

Keep literature releases and product releases separate. Releases that describe products and include some literature about that product are excellent for use by the editor. He has more technical data than he can possibly use and thus can select those that are most appropriate for his readers. Sending published or printed data on a product is a good practice to follow.

But don't let this approach get away from you. An announcement about a product is not an announcement about the literature concerning that product. Some editors may divide the material into two possible press announcements; one for the product, one for the literature. You get two announcements for the effort of writing one. Consider yourself lucky. You might have sent two announcements in the same package and seen either the product or the literature announcement in print—but not both.

DUPLICATE RELEASES ARE NOT TWICE AS GOOD

Some companies send releases that exactly duplicate ones they had sent a half year or a year earlier, and the year before that too. They do it in the hope that they will get new press coverage of an old item. These are generally releases on products and literature.

Once an editor spots this practice he discards all material that comes from that source. If he cannot remember whether he used the release in the past and later finds that he has, he will suspect all other material emanating from that company. As a result, the company's releases on truly new products or literature will not be published.

It is also not a good idea to send a release in duplicate. When this happens because the typists addressing the envelopes lose track of where they left off, the mistake can be excused. One copy is simply discarded. However, when a release is sent one month and a duplicate is sent the following month or several weeks later, it begins to look like a transparent attempt to obtain a second mention of the single item.

PEOPLE IN THE NEWS

An important department in most publications is the one concerning the people in the industry or profession. This "gossip column" keeps readers informed of the movements and achievements of their colleagues, and is one of the most popular items in any journal.

News releases about people will include news of promotions, transfers, honors, awards, title changes, function changes, deaths, and more. There is really no limit to the detail that could be published; only good editorial judgment keeps this within bounds.

News about people should be about people. This may sound redundant, but many press releases issued by industrial companies are less about the people they purport to discuss than about the company or its chief executive. Many such announcements mention that the president of the company announces a number of changes. Wonderful, but for whom? The name of the president appears more often than anyone else's. This type of release, which contains too much unnecessary information, is ripe for the introduction of errors. The president is announced as becoming the new sales manager or production superintendent. This is not what the sender intended.

Give the name of the person, give his new title (never give his old function), and, if appropriate, briefly describe his new duties. Keep it short. Leave out the names of his wife and children and his home address. That's appropriate for the local weekly; it doesn't belong in the business or professional press.

Unless there is a company reorganization, do not combine announcements of promotions and changes of job functions with other news. Some publications keep such data separate and will direct the release to one or the other location, seldom to both. By mixing material the impact is reduced. Some information might even get lost.

BUSINESS GROWTH AND EXPANSION NEWS

If your organization, company, or association is active in an industry it is likely that readers of the appropriate journals are interested in news about your company. They are concerned that you are growing, that you have committed capital expansion plans. They are certainly going to be concerned if you change your address or your telephone number. If they do business with you they are involved with these matters. Such news merits publication, so it will be available to more than the selected customers who receive your mailed announcements.

In addition, it is an excellent way to get positive public exposure with relatively little effort. Use it. Journals of all sorts carry news about suppliers to the industry—news beyond that involved with products, literature, and people.

There is almost no limit to the type of news that is appropriate. Your company may have dedicated a new research center, hosted a Boy Scout convention, donated land to the Nature Conservancy, come to agreement with a labor union, won or lost a union certification election, been honored for its export marketing, begun reorganizing, and so on, and so on, and so on.

Some companies find a favorable reception for news items about major contracts and sales. If this is the case then by all means send out such news to the business press.

You will generally find that the biggest or smallest or most special of something is newsworthy in itself. If your company has made the largest widget, that's news. If it has made the smallest widget, that too is news. These are items of interest to people who use widgets. However, if the company has created a new shop record and turned out a record number of widgets in a given amount of time, that's not news to those outside the company. You're just boasting.

Use your judgment when planning releases of this sort. They have significant public relations value when handled properly— unfortunately, they are seldom handled properly.

EVENTS PAST, PRESENT, AND FUTURE

Without question, one of the most important services a journal can provide its readers is bringing them news of events—past, present, and future. These may merely be lists of future activities of industry associations and societies. Such news may include activities involving seminars conducted by colleges and universities or even by industrial companies and private consulting groups.

An event that has taken place, such as an open house, whether industrial, commercial, or educational, can be of considerable interest to readers. Photographs may be appropriately used here, particularly if the event took place and no one from the business or professional press was in attendance. If only a few press representatives were present other journals that could not have staff personnel attend may be interested in publishing the material.

Events scheduled for the future often receive much better press coverage than events which have ended. Readers may want to participate in future activities. Learning enough about them in advance will enable them to make the necessary plans and arrangements. Keep news releases about events short but do not hesitate to send them to the widest group of publications that you have dealt with in the past and which you know to be interested. Avoid sending such material to journals which have never used your press releases before; they will not publish this as news.

SENDING UNWANTED MATERIAL

If you go through the standard reference sources, such as *Bacon's, Writers' Guide,* and others, you will find that they list some types of material as being accepted by editors. But watch out—they're not always accurate. They make errors in transcribing editors' notations and often list material as acceptable when it is not.

Most editors will not return material sent to them in error by people who used incorrect listings in such directories. The editors have neither the time nor inclination; in fact, most editors are pretty high-handed with material they have not contracted for. If it doesn't fit, it goes out—and is not returned. This is inevitable given the quantity of mail that crosses an editor's desk in one day. It takes a secretary several hours just to open and sort the mail. Under these circumstances sending press clippings, reviews, or materials published in other journals that the editor knows about is fruitless. When the reference source says to query the editor first it generally means just that. The only exceptions are product, literature, personnel, and news releases. If you are looking for items that the publication pays for there are never any exceptions to the admonition to query first.

Don't just send material in the hope that you might be the one person whose material gets published and paid for. If a magazine does not take clippings you are wasting postage in the hope that you have uncovered something worth getting paid for. Likewise for other materials, such as book reviews, letters, and anything else, including, in some instances, product news, news of people, and other similarly conventional items.

If you ever visit an editor's office toward the end of the day take a look at the wastepaper basket. It will probably be overflowing, mostly with material that the editor does not want, will not use, and cannot possibly acknowledge having received.

The Real Junk Mail

Some companies send journals the texts of speeches made by their chief executive officers. This type of submission is neither an article nor a news release. It is simply junk mail, and is treated as such by editors.

A speech of this sort typically covers a presentation made by the CEO before the graduating class of an elementary school, high school, or college. It rarely relates to the business of the company, the publication, or the industry and is usually full of personal reminiscences and advice. It is not publishable material any more than Ernest Hemingway's short stories are publishable in the business and professional press. Submitting a speech of this sort is a waste of everybody's time as well as a waste of the money spent to reproduce the speech, the postage, and the paper.

Sometimes corporate officers testify before congressional committees. Spare the editor the task of plowing through the text to find out that "Senator Drouwzy, from the State of Somnolence," woke up at a "critical point in the presentation." If the material is worth bothering with in the first place, excerpt the key points and send a release of not more than three double-spaced pages. If it is going to be longer throw it out and save the postman the trouble of carrying it to the editor for him to throw out.

PHOTOGRAPHS

Identify Photographs Clearly

If you are planning to send pictures with your press releases, fine. Just remember that the editor will receive lots of other releases with accompanying photos. It does not matter whether you identify the person who appears in the picture on the front or the rear of the photo. It doesn't matter if you print his name and company identification as part of the picture or if you supply this information on an attached label. But be sure to put it there!

Imagine the confusion that is created when an editor receives a press release on seven important promotions in a company, accompanied by seven unidentified photographs. (That's not a far-fetched situation; many release writers seem to forget that the people who have been promoted are not known personally to the editors.) Now consider what happens when pictures are detached from the releases for editing and printing. If they are not identified properly the editor is not the only one in trouble; the printer is confused too. When a printer gets confused he stops working—and deadlines are not met.

One easy solution available to the editor is to simply discard all unidentified pictures. If you have paid for a photographer, for prints, and for postage, and then failed to clearly indicate the person's name and company affiliation, you have thrown your money away.

The same applies for pictures of products or installations or anything else. If the caption is a long one don't paste it onto the back of the photo. The caption goes to the typesetter but the photo does not. Instead, type or print the caption on a separate piece of paper that can be easily detached (torn off) so it can be sent to the typesetter while the editor sizes the picture for use. Because these two pieces are handled separately by the printer, they must be handled separately by the editor. If you lack the clerical help you need to attach captions to photos then make up the caption for the photo and have it reproduced on the front of the photo as part of the print. The editor can easily cut it off.

Identify the company both on the caption and on the photo (if they are to be separated). Do not use flow pens or china markers. When photographs are stacked, the ink comes off the backs of the pictures onto the fronts of other photos—and ruins them. Some rubber-stamp inks are acceptable; others will run, and pencil rubs off. A typed label is best.

Announcements containing photographs printed on the page may be of interest to your customers. However, these are not press releases and they have only limited usefulness to editors. Generally, it is not possible to reproduce a photograph from a printed page. If it is done the loss in quality is tremendous. When a photo is printed it must be broken up into a halftone pattern. Such a pattern does not always pick up well for secondary reproduction.

Most editors will not bother to cut out a photograph and mark it for publication if it is already printed, so don't expect such photographs to be used with your press announcement.

Avoid Creating Holes and Tears

One way to quickly wear out a welcome with an editor is to staple pictures to press releases. When the editor wants to remove the photo he will end up tearing either the release (which he can tape up and use) or the picture (which he cannot use if it is taped together). If you do it once you might be excused. Do it twice and your releases will fill the round file.

Another sure way to reach the round file is to paste pictures to the text of the press release. The pictures will be thrown out every time, and the release will usually go with it. Of course, if you use rubber cement and the release is of genuine interest to the editor you can manage to clog his desk with all sorts of paper that the residue of cement catches on when the editor has to remove the picture. You can be sure that the welcome mat will not be out for you the next time, and that your material will be used infrequently.

Postal employees seem to enjoy testing the packaging of those items marked "fragile" and are especially alert to envelopes marked "*Photos. Do not bend.*" They seem to be challenged by such cautions and feel compelled to prove their ability to "fold, spindle, and mutilate." Place a stiffener in any envelope in which you enclose a photo you would like to see published. If you don't you can be sure that the picture will arrive with a strategically placed crease that cannot be cropped out. Is a lovely white jagged line through the middle of your glossy print what you want? If it isn't you must take precautions to protect the photo.

Even if your photographs arrive on the editor's desk undamaged, remember that the editor has to process the photos through a series of operations. If the photos become damaged during editorial processing (because they are printed on lightweight paper), they will not be usable.

Little Pictures Don't Go Over Big

When major articles are prepared, the editor makes sure that the photographs supplied are of a convenient size. Some people seem to believe that wallet-size photos are appropriate for photos of people. They are, if the photo is to go into a wallet, but are easily lost in a pile of papers.

Some people send contact prints of 35 mm shots thinking they are just fine. They would be fine, if someone could figure out how to find them when they fall into the paper-clip tray.

At the other end of the scale are 8 × 10 prints of people. They too are difficult to work with, although some editors do prefer them, a carryover from the days when smaller prints could not easily be converted to letterpress printing blocks. Nowadays, so many publications are printed offset that a good standard size for pictures of people is 4 × 5, or, if you must, 5 × 7. Since most photos of people are seldom printed larger than 14 picas wide (about 2⅜ inches) an original that is twice the final printed size is good. When it is reduced it becomes sharper than the original.

White margins are needed on all photos. European photographers and, more recently, U.S. ones have started to eliminate the white margins on photos. This may be more attractive but it is inconvenient for publishing purposes. The editor needs to put crop marks on the photos to indicate what portion he wishes to have printed. This tells the printer the limits of the photographic area to be reproduced. Without white margins the editor must place these marks on the face of the subject area and risks obliterating portions of the photo.

A LITTLE GOES A LONG WAY

Sometimes less is more (and more is less). This advice applies for press releases. An editor will usually publish only one product release from one source in a single issue. Sending him more means either that you put off publication of your other product releases or have them discarded. Some editors don't hold product release material from one month to the next, or from week to week. They get too old and out of date.

Send only one release in an envelope. You risk losing everything you send when you send more than one release at a time. This is particularly true for releases from businesses. It is not quite so true for those from associations and societies. If the release the editor sees on top of the pile is not of interest to him he will probably discard the entire package.

Keep releases short. One page is best. If your release is two pages long one page can get lost in the mailroom or on the secretary's desk. If you have to single-space to get all the material in then single-space—but try to keep to a single sheaf of paper.

It is not likely that any single news item that you feel is important will be considered equally important by the editor. You may feel that you require three pages to tell your story; the editor may allow you as little as 100 words—and this is only because his junior editors have not yet developed the necessary skills to condense the material into 50 words.

If the editorial staff is truly under pressure of time they will simply take the first paragraph of your release and edit it, omitting all the rest. Or, they might print only the first sentence, giving you about 15 to 20 words in all and discard the rest. This puts a premium on brevity and clear communication, so you had better get to your point quickly and in terms the reader can comprehend.

Associations and societies can often get away with violating some of these rules. Editors are attuned to the demands placed upon association and society personnel by their directors and will make a little more effort to accommodate to these pressures. Not so with industrial and commercial businesses.

Make sure the release is legible. If this sounds like an unnecessary admonition, please be assured it is not. A light or illegible photocopy can create problems, especially if some of the technical terms used are unfamiliar to the editor. Even if the chief editor knows the terms his editorial assistant may not. The typesetter, who sets type by reading letters, not words, will have a very hard time with light copies.

A little care and consideration of the problems and job of the editor is important in getting him to do your bidding. The editor is willing. If you do your part he will respond by giving you the best he and his publication have to offer.

DON'T MAKE UNREALISTIC REQUESTS

Every once in a while an editor gets a press release with a covering letter and a request that the writer be notified as to when the news item will appear. A postage-paid return post card may be included. An editor simply cannot give you an answer if you make such a request. He neither knows when an item will appear nor will he be able to take the time to establish that fact.

When the item does appear, the editor will not be able to retrieve it from among the hundreds of other, similar items. He would only be able to find a specific item if his publication maintains files to achieve this end. New product publications are virtually the only ones with this type of setup. As for other news items, almost no publication can readily provide this type of information.

In addition, the editor to whom the release and letter are addressed generally does not prepare the material for publication. He is usually a senior-level editor who determines only whether the material is suitable for publication. Someone on his staff, usually a junior editor, processes the material. From there on the senior editor does not have contact with the item, which becomes one of hundreds that go into each and every issue. Finding it is like looking for a needle in a haystack. As for the time it would take, no publisher would allow such profligate expenditure of editorial time.

If you are fortunate enough you will receive a copy of the magazine in which the release is printed along with reader-service inquiries. Most other news items do not have recall value to readers so it is unlikely that you would receive a copy of the final printed version of these releases.

TO WHOM SHOULD YOU ADDRESS RELEASES?

Most PR people would like to be sure their releases reach the proper editorial persons. They are reluctant to simply send a release to a magazine and hope that the mailroom people will direct the contents properly.

This is a needless fear. Business journals rely heavily on material that comes through the mails. Professional publications that publish non-article submissions are similarly dependent. The editor will make a judgment of the value of any mail addressed to the publication unless it obviously belongs to another department, such as circulation or sales. Questionable material goes to the editor and he redirects it accordingly, uses it, or discards it. Nothing gets lost or misplaced or misdirected. Address all general releases to "The Editor." It will get to the one person on the editorial staff who makes the decisions concerning content of the magazine. It could go to the managing editor, an associate editor, a copy editor, or anyone else. It will be routed to the right person regardless of how it is addressed.

If you address the envelope to a specific person you may lose your chance for publication. If your mailing list is not up to date (and whose is?) then you might have used the name of an editor who no longer works for the magazine. In addition, if an editor sees that the name on the envelope is of someone who has not been associated with the magazine for 10 or more years, he may simply throw away the material. This saves him work. If you are not interested enough in his magazine to keep up with changes why should the editor bother about you? You obviously don't value his journal very highly. If you do send material to a particular person, at least spell his name correctly. This is particularly true if the name is on a label or some other form of multiple printing.

MAILING TIPS

Most editors don't care whether you send releases by first class or third class mail, but if you use third class mail don't expect to get a priority publishing date. Third class is quite suitable for sending literature. Postage is expensive and editors are aware that although some material is not particularly timely it is nevertheless truly appropriate for their journals' readers.

Since you are going to send only one item per transmittal you need to save money, but remember that you can expect a timely reaction to your submissions in accordance with the time factors that you build into the transmission of your own material.

CALLING AHEAD

Every editor gets phone calls asking if his journal publishes certain types of material. These are legitimate and possibly desirable inquiries, although they are usually unnecessary. However, when an agency or a client has doubts about the appropriateness of the material one phone call can help.

If you do call about a specific item indicate to the editor that you are planning to send something to him. But don't expect him to commit himself to publish it. He will make his decision when he sees the item. If he decides to publish, so much the better. If not, nothing is really lost.

In a case such as this use first class mail, address the release to the editor personally by name, and prepare a covering letter in which you should refer to your telephone conversation. Get the most mileage out of your effort. It usually pays off.

EDITORS, WHEN SURVEYED, COMPLAINED

In the only survey of its type ever conducted, editors complained that they could not always obtain material of interest to them and could not always get the "meat" out of the material. This was found in a survey conducted early in 1978 by the National Bureau of Standards and the American Business Press. The great majority of the editors who participated in the survey were complimentary concerning the range and quality of information produced and provided by NBS. They continually cited, however, the enormous volume of material they received from NBS and from other sources.

To quote from the summary of results of the survey:

Despite considerable diversity of opinion on a variety of subjects, a composite view of editor preferences clearly emerged from their responses. These business publication editors stated that in order for the information to be of the greatest possible use, it should be presented in a form that can be quickly scanned for items of interest. It enhances the process if the material is attractive in appearance and is set in a type size large enough to be easily read.

Brief, concise, summary reports are best, arranged in an indexed format that makes it easy to identify subjects of interest. In all cases, the names, addresses, and telephone numbers of contacts should be furnished for each item, to facilitate follow-up.

Finally, the material should be written in a nontechnical style, explaining the significance of the items and providing the editor with an opportunity to assess its importance in relation to subscriber interests.

The following were among the findings:

The editors displayed clear preference for material that was timely, brief, and offered on an exclusive basis. They valued less strongly variety, detail, and the existence of illustrations. Concerning subject matter, they regarded as most useful information on new products, scientific and technical reports, and descriptions of policies and programs. Less useful was material dealing with conferences, new publications, speeches, congressional testimony, annual reports, personnel matters, and contract awards.

Regarding the usefulness of 17 sample items of NBS output contained in the NBS packet, the editors expressed strongest preference for news releases and a document called "Monthly Highlights" that consists of a collection of brief program reports, topped with descriptive headlines and organized under subject headings.

Other preferred items included the feature articles, technical illustrated staff reports, and a page of "news briefs" that appear in the NBS monthly magazine. Also ranked in the upper half of the preference scale were a report on a technical subject written in a straightforward and readable style, and a four-page report containing brief accounts of technical conferences to be held at NBS.

Considered less useful by the editors were such items as the *Publications Newsletter*, set in densely packed, small type and material that is either strictly technical in nature or is presented in the form of pamphlets intended for consumers and homeowners. . . .

What these business publication press editors say they most need are indexes, or guides, to help sort through the tremendous amount of information they must process daily so that they can identify subjects of interest to their specific and specialized audience of readers.

The results of the survey may not be surprising to most editors. Indeed, they confirm the suggestions made to NBS by the American Business Press staff members before the survey was made.

This, in a nutshell, is what you have just read in this chapter. Hopefully, you now know the "how" and "why" of the conclusions reached in this survey.

15

advertisers do get special treatment

"EVERYBODY," the expression goes, "knows that advertisers are favored."

Yes, in the business press they are. And if there is advertising in the professional journals, they are favored there too.

Be realistic. Favoring an advertiser is not prostitution. What is unacceptable and immoral is using editorial space as unpaid advertising. The reader should not be subjected, in an editorial column, to the commercial message of an advertiser, worded the way an advertiser would word his promotional matter.

Another practice that occurs outside North America regularly, and infrequently on this continent, is the "trading" of editorial space in exchange for paid advertising space. Most European advertisers expect to receive good editorial mention on a quid pro quo basis when they purchase advertising.

But what if an advertiser has something of genuine value to impart to an industry? Isn't he the most likely source for news of something new and interesting? Aren't the advertisers the source of much of the equipment used in an industry? Aren't they the participants in and supporters of the trade and professional associations of the industry? The people who work for those companies are known to the operating and management people in the industry. So an advertiser's concepts of design and implementation affect other people working in the business or profession.

It is perfectly logical that an advertiser will have something of value to offer the industry, and that he should announce it first in the publications which serve that industry. Advertisers are not so much the favored sources of articles and news as they are the *basic* sources.

ADVERTISERS ARE PART OF THE INDUSTRY

Advertisers are as much a part of an industry as the people they sell to. Their economic and personal fortunes rise and fall with the economic conditions of the industry they serve. In fact, there are some advertisers who sell virtually nothing as a direct result of their advertising. Yet they continue to advertise to maintain visibility in the industry.

Some companies feel obligated to assist the business media in bringing news to the industry. Their advertising is one way they express their gratitude to the media for aiding them in reaching the industry when they have non-advertising approaches that they wish to take to reach their market, as for example, by means of technical articles.

Successful companies that do not advertise and do not attend technical meetings and conventions but participate in trade shows are not popular with editors or publishers. They are ready to sell products but are not ready to help customers solve problems. They too want to have articles concerning their business appear in the leading business and professional journals—but they have not supported the industry by supporting these journals. Should editors give them the same consideration they accord advertisers? Most editors would agree that they should not.

Readers Know Advertised Products and Companies

Approaching the question of favoring advertisers from another point of view, we find that readers are more familiar with the names of advertisers and with their products. Whatever some people believe about advertising, the fact remains that ads tend, over the long term, to create a sense of familiarity. We welcome someone we know and we know advertisers.

When an advertiser's name appears in connection with an article, the reader knows this has a potential connection with sales. If the article is a story about a case history, for instance, the reader knows that he can obtain benefits similar to those described for the user of the advertised product. Since credibility has already been established the reader is not fearful of claims from someone he may have never dealt with before.

If the advertiser's chief engineer has written an article, with a byline clearly naming him, many potential customers and past customers will respond to the appearance of an old friend. He may be known personally to many of the readers. Aren't you more interested in what your friends have to say than in what a stranger might say? We all are.

If the byline does not carry a familiar name, the name that is familiar may be that of the company or organization. The company, then, is the friend in the person of the individual who has been in contact, in the field, with the reader. This person is the company, not just its representative. Looking at the byline in this manner we can read it as the company—local representative in mind—followed by the name of a colleague of the local representative. Another welcome by the reader.

ADVERTISING AS A COURTESY

Some corporate managements believe they should "repay" a journal which publishes an article that it has prepared or has an interest in. (This is not an attempt to influence the decision of whether or not to publish an article; the article has already been accepted for publication.) Such companies feel an obligation to show appreciation, and do so by buying advertising space. Companies may ask for space in the same issue in which the editorial mention occurs. Most reputable publishers and editors try to avoid this, because it may look suspicious. This type of advertising should appear subsequent to the editorial, not concurrently and not earlier.

DON'T PROMISE SPACE FOR EDITORIAL

The quickest way to get an article idea rejected is to write an editor or telephone him and promise that if you get a story published and the response is good your company or client will advertise.

The idea that you can trade editorial for advertising won't work in North America. In the United States and Canada the business press tends to separate its editorial and advertising so that one is not dependent upon the other. As noted, they are not always completely independent but their dependency is not tied together on a quid pro quo basis as it is with the trade media in Europe, Latin America, and elsewhere.

If you have a story to tell, the editor will be interested. If your story is not worth telling, but you are the publication's largest advertiser, the editor will try to dissuade you from publishing something that he feels will affect your company's image adversely. He will likely reject what you offer for his editorial pages. If there is a toss-up as to whether to accept a story from an advertiser or a comparable one from a non-advertiser the rules promulgated above will apply.

ADVERTISING IS HANDLED BY ADVERTISING REPRESENTATIVES

The editor is not the advertising salesman nor is he the publisher. As he views it, if you advertise he will offer you the same opportunity to present your story in his journal as if you don't advertise, and vice versa.

Advertising agencies that write to editors and try to obtain favorable editorial treatment by promising to buy advertising space know they are being dishonest. They should write directly to the publisher or the sales representative. They are experienced enough to know that space representatives, not editors, handle space. But they really aren't looking to buy advertising space; rather they're using a ploy to gain free publicity.

Sometimes an agency will try to sweeten its offer by saying that it will consider advertising if it gets a good response from the editorial coverage. This is also not valid and they know it. Response from space advertising is seldom as good as response from editorial. They would do better by offering the material to the editor and asking only that any responses be directed to the agency and not to the client. If they choose to measure response they can do so.

Readers trust that editors will protect them from unscrupulous non-advertisers and even from unscrupulous advertisers who would use the editorial pages improperly; that is, for the benefit of the advertiser and not for the benefit of the reader. The reader trusts the editor to act in his behalf in assembling news and data of value to him. If the editor violates that trust he will lose readers, circulation, and eventually good advertising volume that he depends on.

16

---

merchandising the article

MERCHANDISING YOUR ARTICLE means reprinting it (or having the magazine reprint it for you) for use as sales promotion literature. An article that appears in a journal enjoys the prestige of that journal. When you merchandise your article you are leaning on that journal; you are subsuming for yourself the standing that the journal enjoys in its business or professional community. It no longer is your article; it is an article about you. You can stand taller than the organization that does not have such an article to represent itself.

Because of the esteem in which the business and professional press is (rightfully) held, your article places you on a higher level that if you had never had such an article published. What has been published about your product, your idea, your service, your organization, your whatever is considered factual and stated with propriety. You have not made any claims for yourself; the journal has made them for you.

The follow-up value is immensely prestigious. This is why so many companies make such a tremendous effort and expend such considerable sums of money to get into print. An advertisement is a commercial message; an article is a dispassionate evaluation by someone else, even when it has your name on it.

WHEN WILL THE ARTICLE APPEAR?

Whether yours is a full-length article, a series, or just a press release, don't ask the editor when it will appear. He will volunteer that information if it is important to let you know. Otherwise, he probably won't be able to tell you for certain.

Until a magazine issue is fully assembled the editor is not really sure of what will appear. Advertising has claims of priority which an editor cannot change, although he may influence them a bit. At the last moment an ad may come in that requires that some editorial matter be canceled or postponed. A mechanical problem may arise that requires the editor to "pull" the article. Or a threat in the legal area may cause an article to be canceled at the last moment, when it has already been committed to specific pages of a specific issue.

Remember, too, the editor is not working for you. If you burden him with paperwork you are looking for problems. Pestering an editor will not endear you to him.

It is up to you to follow the publication of your material. In the average issue of an average business magazine there may be as many as 100 to 150 different items that have been contributed in one form or another. The editor cannot possibly select the one item you are interested in and make a special effort to notify you of its appearance.

TIE-IN PROMOTIONS

Every editor knows why you want to know when a specific item will appear—and is sympathetic to your circumstances. You almost certainly will have other promotional material to tie in with the article or release and wish to have it all neatly coordinated.

You may want to tie in your article or release with a business convention, a trade show, a technical conference, a sales meeting, an annual meeting, and other such meetings, conventions, conferences, and shows. Plan to reprint enough copies of the article to cover your needs for such activities during the course of one, two, or more years. Try to avoid planning a specific appearance of an article for a specific occasion; wait until the article has actually appeared before you plan a tie-in promotion with it.

USING AN ARTICLE AS SALES LITERATURE

In addition to their use as direct mail sales literature, reprints are useful as inserts in sales catalogs. They work quite well in technical and management proposals, in sales proposals, and in other similar documents. They offer assurance to your customer of your stability and competence. He is likely to be impressed that your subject matter was important enough to the industry to be published in the industry's prestigious journal.

Salesmen can leave copies with customers. When they do that it implies that no sales message would be quite as effective as the non-selling message contained in the article. That is the best type of selling: allowing the customer to convince himself that you are the best company to do business with.

Reprints of articles have been used effectively when dealing with the financial community. Many analysts have only a sketchy knowledge of the business of a company whose securities they are responsible for recommending. An article can help to show where your company stands in a particular industry or a particular technology. Because an article is news it is easy reading. Analysts can get a complex message very quickly, in a simple form.

GETTING REPRINTS

What are reprints? Reprints are copies of published material. Reprints carry the name of the journal and generally a copyright notice that the material is reprinted by permission. If advertisements were interspersed with the editorial matter, the advertising is removed.

You can normally purchase reprints from the magazine or you can have them reprinted by your own printer. If you get them from the magazine you will generally pay a standard commercial price that is about in line with what you would pay for other printing.

You will find that ordering them from the magazine can save a lot of time and effort on your part. Even if it does cost a few pennies more it is worth not having the nuisance of handling it yourself.

If material has appeared in color you probably would pay far more for reprints if you do not purchase them from the publication. They have already done the work of processing the artwork for color separation in printing and have already absorbed that cost in the cost of publishing the journal itself. If you do not purchase such color reprints from the magazine you will certainly have to go through the process of creating separate color plates for printing, which can be very costly.

In addition, if you have copies printed by your own printer you will have to wait until the magazine is sent to you and you may have to generate new mechanical layouts from the material which has already appeared in the magazine. In this case you will have to take some steps to avoid infringing upon copyright of the publication. You must obtain permission to reprint, which you can get only from the magazine's publishers (either the editor or someone whose job it is to handle reprints). If you do not have permission in writing, do not attempt to reprint. The new U.S. copyright law has far more stringent reprint regulations than the old one it recently replaced, and the old one did not allow reprinting without permission.

If you receive verbal permission from the editor be sure to confirm it in writing before you reprint. If the editor does not send you a letter giving permission send him one confirming your verbal permission. Keep a copy in your files. When you have copies of the reprint available, send the editor at least two copies and inform him as to the number of copies you have had printed.

Some magazines and journals do not give permission to reprint under any circumstances. You cannot get around this refusal.

Such publications insist that all reprints from their journals be published under their direction, and they expect payment from you for those reprints.

If you have an article and you wish to have the magazine's cover included in your reprint this is most economically done by the magazine, and even then it will not be cheap. If the cover is in color the costs of reprinting will be even more expensive. Nevertheless, many purchasers of reprints find that this use of a magazine's front cover is extremely effective in lending credibility to the reprint.

YOU MAY COPY FOR PERSONAL USE

Do be very careful that you do not plan to reprint an article and then sell copies. That is in violation of the copyright law. The new copyright law forbids the copying of copyright material for other than personal use by the one individual who does the copying. The copied material may not be used for any other purpose, not even to distribute to friends to show them your work. The copied items cannot legally be shown to a client or customer. Copied material may be used for one purpose only: your own personal reference. It cannot be legally sent to salesmen just to show them what has been published. If you want to do that get more copies from the magazine or get written permission to make such copies.

Warnings against unauthorized copying of copyright material have been issued by all manufactueres of copying equipment. Some have these warnings posted prominently on all their office copiers. Violation of these warnings can be a serious offense and presumes an intent to violate the law. You can get into a lot of trouble. Although you will not likely go to jail over this matter financially it can be costly.

REVIEWING COMPLETED LAYOUT PAGES

This discussion of review really does belong here in the chapter on merchandising. A review of completed layout pages is not really a review of the article; it is a review of the physical layout and the placement of the components. Generally, you will want to know what the article's physical layout is in order to plan your merchandising and marketing literature around it. It helps to know how many pages are actually required for the reprinted article.

Editors are normally quite reluctant to send advance copies of pages. They cannot guarantee that the article will be printed in exactly that form. Also, if the pages have been laid out in the journal in such a manner that they will require modification to create a promotion piece, the space occupied in the magazine may not provide you with adequate guidance for planning the promotion piece.

On the other hand it just might work. Even if it works only to a limited extent it may be of value.

If you are planning to have an article reprinted and it must be coordinated with other promotional material you may want to know enough about the final form so you can plan your marketing effort concurrently with the printing of the journal. This enables you to gain considerable time, possibly as much as three or four weeks in the case of a monthly.

17

---

writing for money

THERE ARE MANY fine books available that tell you how you can get paid for your writing. However, very few of the more than 6,000 major and 30,000 minor business and professional publications pay for articles. Those that do will pay only to bona fide free-lancers; only a few will reimburse industrial, scientific, or business writers who are employed by the companies and organizations they are writing about.

If you are a professional writer working for a company don't expect to receive payment from a journal. Such authors may be paid only under special circumstances; for example, when they do work for the publication that would normally be done by staff editors. This is, however, very unusual (although I know from personal experience how nice it is to receive payment from two sources for the same work). Be advised, however, that such writing will require many hours to earn the fee.

Payment policies of journals will vary. Do not assume that because the payment policy of the journal is said in a writing market guide book to be so much per page that you will automatically receive that amount. If it is your job to write articles, as a professional public relations consultant, or if you are paid for other work and the articles develop as a consequence of such work, you may be permitted the time to write the article upon completion of your regular work. If you have been assigned by your company to write an article at the request of the editor of a journal your company or organization may be pleased to have you devote company working time to the article. In any case, you should not ask for payment from the magazine.

PAYMENT BY YOUR OWN COMPANY

Some companies use payments to their employees as an incentive to write. This payment is not for writing done in lieu of other project work but in addition to it.

I know of companies that paid their engineers to write articles with no prospect of publication. The engineers worked on their own time but were compensated at a good rate, almost equal to their on-the-job hourly rate of pay. Then, when the articles were completed, they were handed over to the public relations manager to "place" them. Of course, none of these articles ever came close to meeting the requirements of the publications that the marketing manager wanted them to appear in. To be suitable for publication they would have had to be rewritten extensively. The public relations managers, advertising managers, and technical publications managers had never been informed which engineer was asked to write on which subject. As a result, such endeavors were a waste of personal effort and a waste of company funds.

On the other hand, if the marketing manager of any one of these companies had asked his public relations manager to solicit interest from the various journals in the field he might have assured the engineers that their efforts would be rewarded not only with money but with publication as well. The engineers would then have started to work on those projects that were certainly of interest to readers of those journals.

Many companies have policies of paying their nonwriting employees for articles as long as the company name is associated with the article. Such articles might be on any subject, even ones not appropriate for business or professional journals, but more suitable for consumer publications or newspapers.

In well-managed companies which have large engineering staffs and in which the technical nature of the material is so abstruse that it precludes intelligent writing by surrogate writers, public relations or technical writers are assigned to help the engineers and scientists. The PR or technical writers help with the preparation of visual materials, work with the manuscript, and so on. In general, the PR and technical writers are experienced and skilled in publications work and are familiar with all the steps that pertain to the production of a magazine. Under these circumstances, the engineering writers would write on their own time, for which they would be paid, but would spend some on-the-job time with the publications specialists.

When such articles are completed (usually more rapidly and more carefully because of this help) they are really ready to be published. The magazine or journal editor will work with the public relations person or writing consultant, not with the author himself. Working relationships between professionals in the same "business" make everyone's tasks easier. The results certainly prove that this approach works well. Companies without such skilled personnel do not get as many articles published as those that have internal or external help available for their authors.

Some companies pay technical personnel who write articles upon acceptance of the article by the publication. If that is the case in your company get to know your professional contacts in your own company. Some companies pay when the article is in a form that an editor finds acceptable, even though the editor has not yet committed himself to publish the material. Others pay upon completion of a manuscript, in almost any condition. This is the best deal for a writer who is not dedicated but who can string words together fast.

PAYMENT BY MAGAZINES

Write First, Get Paid Later

Magazines that pay for articles will do so only after you deliver the merchandise. Some magazines pay upon receipt of solicited material, others pay upon publication only. Some pay upon acceptance—although acceptance means that you may have to wait a month or two to find out if your material is likely to be published. Some magazines have been known to pay upon acceptance, and then never publish the material. In short, policies differ among journals. To find out what policies pertain to a particular magazine just ask the editor.

Under normal circumstances, there is no such thing as partial payment. You are not under contract to write; you have an agreement with your editor, which may or may not be in writing, that your article might (repeat, might) be acceptable. You have no guarantees. (If you have a contract for a number of articles ignore this book. You are in a league by yourself.) You will be paid when the editor decides that your submission meets his publication and payment policies—you won't be paid any sooner than that.

Don't Start Until the Word "Go"

Don't do anything until the editor tells you to start, whether you are writing for money or writing for publicity. You will waste time and effort with a premature start. Of course, in order to have made a proposal you must have had something in hand or in mind. To do more than you have already done up to that point without an expression of interest by the editor is unwise. You might wish to proceed if you feel that you can "sell" the article to another editor with whom you have not yet made a contact.

This admonition applies whether you are a free-lancer or whether you are in the employ of a company. As a professional you will already have learned this lesson. However, if circumstances force you to proceed before you should, do as little as possible and try to limit what you must do to work that will probably not have to be changed after you have negotiated successfully with an editor.

Too many corporate managers are unaware that the writing of any article is the last and least part of the work of putting an article into print. The vast amount of work is completed before any word goes down on paper. Research must be completed, sources verified, data checked and rechecked, all before you can even formulate an outline. Yet, some managers will tell you to do everything short of submitting the article before you even know if there is a market. You will have to determine how to work within such an environment.

You Won't Get Rich

No business or professional journal pays enough to make you rich. You can make a living, but that is about all. The extra money you might earn as an honorarium for writing is always welcome but seldom munificent.

Business and professional magazines will pay up to $100 per page; most of them pay considerably less. A rate of $50 to $75 per page is normal. A very few pay a rate higher than $100 per page. Payment of $400 or $500 for an assignment by an editor or from a company is about as high as you will find. This rate has not changed very much, even with inflation, over the past several years, and it is not likely to change very much in the next few years either.

MARKETING TO SEVERAL PUBLICATIONS

You can make some additional money by (1) dividing your topic, and (2) dividing your market.

When you research your material, you will come across a great deal of information that is not suitable for the single article you have in mind. You probably will have data suitable for several articles, each of which could appear in a different journal serving a different market and reaching a different group of readers. Therefore, there's the possibility of earning a fee from each of several sources.

Divide your material into the various topics that you feel offer promise of good return. Market those topics. Market them wherever you can, to the journals and to other clients.

If you work for a company and the company pays for articles, suggest that you would like to write two, three, or even four more articles. You might get paid for each. You can then offer different articles to the same journal, or a series of related articles to one journal, all for the same research effort and for a little more writing effort.

By dividing your market you can offer editors of journals in different fields material appropriate to the discipline represented by each journal. An example of this approach is the story of a playground project in California. A free-lance author offered articles to magazines in the nursery school field, the municipal government field, and the paper industry and to psychology and women's shelter (consumer) journals. He got an excellent reception from all of them. Even if he had been paid only $200 per article (and he got more than that from most of his submissions), he would have written five articles for the effort of assembling data for one, and received at least $1,000. He spent less than two weeks on the entire venture.

You may think this is fine and dandy, but only for free-lancers. Well, it is just what professional public relations people get paid by their employers for doing. They try to get the greatest mileage out of their work and the work of their corporate personnel. Companies in the packaging field, as an example, send out stories to the journals which specialize in packaging, but also get their stories printed in journals which specialize in the product areas of the items which are packaged. As many as 30 or even 40 different articles can be generated from a single effort!

index